EMOTIONAL INTELLIGENCE IN LOVE AND RELATIONSHIPS

The Key to Build Happier and Healthier Relationships. Improve Your Social Skills, Empathy, and Learn How to Manage Your Emotions

By

ALI KERR

©Copyright 2022 All Right Reserved.

This document is geared in the direction of giving precise and also trustworthy info when it comes to the subject and concern covered. The publication is offered with the concept that the author is not required to make accountancy, formally allowed, or otherwise qualified services. If advice is needed, lawful, or specialist, a practiced individual in the profession should be gotten.

From a Statement of Concepts that was accepted and accepted similarly by a Board of the American Bar Organization and a Board of Publishers and Associations, in no way is it legal to duplicate, duplicate, or send any part of this record in either electronic means or printed format. Recording of this magazine is strictly forbidden and also any storage space of this file is not allowed unless with created authorization from the publisher. All civil liberties booked.

The details provided herein are specified to be honest and also consistent because any obligation, in terms of inattention or otherwise, by any usage or abuse of any plans, procedures, or instructions consisted of within is the individual and also utter responsibility of the recipient viewers. Under no conditions will certainly any legal obligation or blame be held against the publisher for any adjustment, damages, or monetary loss as a result of the information herein, either straight or indirectly.

Particular writers have all copyrights not held by the author.

The info here is provided for educational objectives exclusively, as well as is universal as so. The presentation of the details is without agreement or any kind of guarantee assurance.

The hallmarks that are made use of are without any authorization, as well as the magazine of the hallmark lacks permission or backing by the trademark owner. All trademarks, as well as brands within this publication, are for clarifying objectives and also are possessed by the propritors themselves, not affiliated with this document.

ISBN: 9798448495540

Table of Contents

- WHAT IS EMOTIONAL INTELLIGENCE 7
- WHY IS EMOTIONAL INTELLIGENCE IMPORTANT? 15
- UNDERSTANDING YOUR PARTNER'S EMOTION . 25
- IS LOW EMOTIONAL INTELLIGENCE AFFECTING YOUR RELATIONSHIP? 39
- MANAGING YOUR EMOTIONS IN A RELATIONSHIP 53
- EMOTIONAL INTELLIGENCE AND MANAGING RELATIONSHIPS 67
- EMOTIONAL INTELLIGENCE: MAKING LOVE LAST 77
- EMOTIONAL INTELLIGENCE IN LOVE AND INTIMATE RELATIONSHIP 89
- IMPROVING FAMILY RELATIONSHIPS WITH EMOTIONAL INTELLIGENCE 103
- HOW TO NURTURE EMOTIONAL INTELLIGENCE IN RELATIONSHIPS 117
- WHAT ACTIONS AND BEHAVIORS WILL MAKE OUR RELATIONSHIP HEALTHIER? 125
- HOW CAN WE PREVENT CRITICISM, MANIPULATION, AND BLAME GAMES IN RELATIONSHIPS? 137
- HOW TO DEVELOP AND EXPRESS EMPATHY FOR YOUR PARTNER. 147
- CONCLUSION 155

WHAT IS EMOTIONAL INTELLIGENCE

Emotional intelligence is the capacity to recognize, control, and assess emotions. The ability to perceive and name one's own emotions and control and use those emotions for tasks such as thinking and problem solving is referred to as emotional intelligence. It also comprises the ability to control one's emotions, including self-regulation and the ability to aid others.

How you perceive and express emotions, like other human characteristics, is a result of both nature and nurture: your genetic legacy and the many experiences you've had since birth. According to some personality psychologists, traits like agreeableness and even charisma can more accurately describe emotional intelligence. A person with a high level of charisma, for example, is socially adept and can read a room quickly. Depending on how a particular day unfolds, you're likely to feel various feelings throughout the day: joy, frustration, happiness, melancholy, and anxiety.

Perhaps you are someone who readily displays their emotions. Maybe you prefer to keep them to yourself. In either case, your emotions have a significant impact on your actions. And how successfully you manage your daily life is influenced by your conduct, words, actions, and facial expressions.

You presumably engage with many people in various settings every day, including family members, neighbors, coworkers, and strangers. These encounters might occur in person or online, be brief or lengthy, and be commonplace or meaningful.

The most significant ones should, in theory, make you feel fulfilled and connected. However, you may occasionally feel betrayed and alone due to your actions. The other individual may share your feelings or react in an entirely different way.

People vary in their ability to recognize emotions in themselves and others and their ability to put that knowledge to good use. Emotional intelligence can have a startling impact on our lives, affecting everything from our ability to form long-term friendships and love relationships to excel in school and seek meaningful employment that gives us a sense of purpose.

HOW TO ASSESS EMOTIONAL INTELLIGENCE

The two most popular such assessments are self-report tests and ability tests. Because they are the most straightforward to administer and evaluate, **self-report tests** are the most prevalent. Respondents to these assessments rate their conduct in response to questions or remarks. A test-taker might disagree, somewhat disagree, agree, or strongly agree with a statement such as "I often feel like I understand how others are experiencing."

Ability tests involve having people respond to events before evaluating their talents. People are routinely asked to exhibit their abilities, which a third party then evaluates.

COMPONENTS OF EMOTIONAL INTELLIGENCE

According to Daniel Goleman (author of the best-selling book Emotional Intelligence), emotional intelligence (EQ) contains five components

- **Self-awareness**
- **Self-regulation**
- **Empathy**

- **Motivation**
- **Social skills**

The components of this paradigm are organized by complexity, with the most fundamental operations at the bottom and the most complicated processes at the top. The lowest levels, for example, are concerned with sensing and expressing emotion, whereas higher levels necessitate greater conscious engagement and concern for emotion regulation.

1. **Self-awareness**

Self-awareness is the ability to recognize and name your emotions and the bodily feelings that accompany them—both positive and negative. This may appear simple, yet tuning in to emotion can be difficult for some. We may have been taught that great emotion, whether it's grief, anger, or anything else that makes us "emotional," is a sign of weakness. As a result, we keep it hidden. On the other hand, if we feel out of control and seek treatment from a mental health expert to understand our feelings, society may look down on us. Even today, going to a "shrink" carries a stigma, even though seeking help when you need it is a fantastic way to enhance your mental health and EQ.

To become emotionally intelligent, you must first be able to recognize and accept your feelings and the source of those emotions, rather than brushing them under the rug.

2. Self-Regulation

While we may not be able to control our reactionary emotions completely, we may learn to manage them more effectively. Our responses to adversity are vital to self-regulation.

For example, instead of reacting angrily, you may spend five minutes learning a breathing technique before reacting to the circumstance with practice. Being non-reactive in a stressful situation needs practice, but learning to self-regulate in almost every setting is possible.

3. **Empathy**

Empathy is the ability to comprehend and perceive the feelings and viewpoints of others. We live in such a distracted world nowadays. I can't help but observe how individuals of all ages are glued to their smartphones rather than engaging with friends and family who are right there whenever I'm in a public location like a restaurant or park! Although our everyday "screen habits" have made it more difficult to glance up, interact, and engage, this isn't a new problem.

Empathy is a necessity for emotional intelligence, and it includes physically tuning into individuals around us to notice and comprehend facial expressions, postures, gestures, tone, and more.

4. **Motivation**

Self-motivated people are more positive, more effective leaders, and more successful. Examining your motivations for wanting to attain goals, being able to defer gratification, and continually seeking to improve are all examples of self-motivation. More motivated people are more resilient when things don't go as planned. Emotional intelligence is key to success. In terms of career, personal objectives, or health, the emotionally intelligent individual understands the need for self-motivation.

5. Social skills

Recognizing somebody's feelings is one thing, but being able to interact with them in light of that information is another. People with good social skills form strong bonds with others and perform well in the workplace, particularly in positions of leadership or teamwork.

WHY IS EMOTIONAL INTELLIGENCE IMPORTANT?

Emotional intelligence (EQ) is important for professional achievement and mutually gratifying personal relationships; emotional intelligence (EQ) is important. EQ enables people to look after their well-being and the well-being of others. You'll find it easier to form deeper relationships, attain professional success, and realize your career and personal goals if you have a high level of emotional intelligence. Emotions are a component of who we are, and the EQ is at the center of who we are.

Emotionally intelligent people can inspire and lead others. As a result, they will be able to maintain healthy connections while also being successful at work. In our personal lives, as well.

- "Do you have any idea what emotion you're experiencing?
- Can you control your emotions without allowing them to overwhelm you?

- Are you able to inspire yourself to complete tasks? Do you have the ability to detect and respond to others' emotions?

You have most likely mastered some or all of the emotional intelligence abilities if you responded yes to these questions.

Emotional intelligence enhances our potential for resilience, motivation, empathy, reasoning, stress management, communication, and our ability to understand and navigate various social situations and disputes by generating the confluence where intellect and emotion meet. EQ is important, and cultivating it can help you live a better, more fulfilling life.

Emotional intelligence can lead us down the path to a satisfied and happy existence by providing a framework to apply intelligence standards to emotional reactions and recognize that these responses may be rationally consistent or inconsistent with particular views about emotion.

People with greater EQ are better equipped to work in teams, deal with change, and deal with stress, which helps them achieve business goals. Interns and supervisors with greater

EQ are better able to work in teams, deal with change, and handle stress, allowing them to achieve corporate goals faster.

You eat well, sleep well, and exercise regularly, but what about your emotional health? Emotional intelligence, specifically.

EMOTIONAL INTELLIGENCE BENEFITS YOU, YOUR CAREER, AND YOUR RELATIONSHIPS.

Beyond your emotional well-being, emotional intelligence has value. Higher EQ is linked to better health, relationships, and professional performance. We all know that brilliant individuals aren't necessarily successful or happy. You probably know someone smart intellectually yet socially uncomfortable and unemployed or unmarried.

Employers increasingly favor emotional intelligence over academic skills in today's modern, adaptive workplace.

How can we make substantial progress if we don't accept our starting point? A destination is worthless without knowing where we're going. Personal and professional success requires emotional intelligence, enhancing interpersonal connections, managing stress and improving motivation, or refining decision-making abilities.

EQ AFFECTS FOUR AREAS OF YOUR LIFE.

1) Physical health

If you can't control your stress levels, it might cause major health issues. Unmanaged stress can elevate blood pressure, depress the immune system, increase the risk of heart attack and stroke, cause infertility, and hasten the aging process. Learning how to manage stress is the first step in increasing emotional intelligence.

The impacts of stress on health are at the heart of most research linking emotional intelligence to good health.

2) Your Mental health

Better relationships and less stress result from increased emotional intelligence. Lower emotional intelligence is linked to increased stress and loneliness. Stress out of control can negatively influence your mental health, making you subject to anxiety and despair. You'll be more prone to mood swings if you can't understand and manage your emotions, and you'll feel lonely and isolated if you can't create close relationships.

3) Your work performance

Most people regard successful CEOs and competent managers to be quite intelligent. While many CEOs are likely to score above average on a normal IQ test, intelligence isn't the only element in professional success. In reality, EQ is even more important than intelligence. In fact, according to one study, emotional intelligence is twice as crucial as intellectual quotient and technical skills combined for all vocations.

With very few exceptions, a job entails some amount of interaction with other people. As a result, it's no surprise that emotional intelligence impacts professional performance.

Most research linking emotional intelligence to professional performance has been conducted on doctors, nurses, and other medical professionals. This link is self-evident: excellent doctors require empathy, consistent self-motivation to avoid burnout, and the ability to self-regulate emotions in a high-stress setting that frequently entails life-or-death decisions. Emotional intelligence is also required for those working in the health coaching field to connect with their customers.

On the other hand, emotional intelligence corresponds with workplace performance regardless of career. Emotional intelligence may assist you in navigating the social intricacies of the workplace, leading and motivating people, and achieving professional success. Many employers now consider emotional intelligence as significant as technical aptitude when evaluating job prospects and require EQ testing before hiring.

4) **Your relationships**

It's hardly unexpected that high EQ and good interpersonal relationships go hand in hand. If you have EQ, you can digest negative feedback in a way that benefits both you and others. In both toddlers and adults, emotional intelligence predicts positive connections. Compassion is developed by becoming more aware of your own and others' feelings. In the heat of the moment, being able to self-regulate intense emotions assures that you won't default to something nasty (that you'll likely regret).

Personal and professional success depends on emotional intelligence. Understanding and controlling your emotions will help you better express yourself and understand people. This improves your ability to communicate and develop relationships both professionally and personally. It can aid with academic and professional success, strengthen relationships, and improve communication skills, to name a few benefits.

Emotional intelligence is required for genuine interpersonal connections. EQ is about controlling emotions to increase job performance and, as a result, assisting people in remaining calm and thinking logically to develop positive relationships and achieve their objectives. There is an irrefutable link between emotional intelligence and how senior executives manage their employees: managers with higher emotional intelligence can manage stress and recognize and resolve stress in others.

EMOTIONAL INTELLIGENCE STRESS MANAGEMENT

When we think of emotional intelligence in stress management and connection building, we can link emotional intelligence abilities and job performance. Stress management has a good impact on job commitment and satisfaction. Employees with advanced emotional intelligence talents have the drive and capacity to develop and sustain high-quality interactions in the workplace.

Those with high EQ are better prepared to manage disagreements and maintain relationships than those with low to moderate EQ. Organizations increasingly value employees who can adapt to change and respond effectively. Individual and group EQ affect job performance. The positive impact of EQ on coping with events and completing duties grows as a person advances in a firm.

We all have busy days; it's natural and manageable with the right tools. Having high Emotional Intelligence is recognizing bad emotions and reacting effectively to prevent them from escalating. Uncontrolled or misread emotions may increase our susceptibility to stress, worry, and despair.

Emotional intelligence skills can help people deal with negative emotions like stress and replace them with good ones. Inability to confront and manage stress can deteriorate one's mental health, affecting physical health.

Researchers studying the social, psychological, and medical aspects of stress have found that dealing with negative emotions helps reduce poor psychological and physical health outcomes.

UNDERSTANDING YOUR PARTNER'S EMOTION

Understanding emotions can help you have better relationships, be happier, and communicate more effectively. Recognizing and understanding our own emotions can help us recognize and understand others'. It affects our ability to communicate in both personal and professional settings. Individuals with higher emotional intelligence are more inclined to approach workplace communication, specifically workplace conflict resolution, collaboratively, working together with others to attain a mutually acceptable outcome. How we manage our emotions and our understanding of others' emotions affects our professional interactions.

A romantic relationship is frequently built on an emotional bond with a partner, but aspects of that bond may be lost as the relationship progresses. It might not be easy to put in the effort required to sustain a strong friendship as life takes over. One of the most common concerns is a lack of comprehension of one's partner's feelings. This can be a two-fold problem: you may have trouble understanding your partner's demands, and your partner may believe you don't understand them. Each circumstance generates questions and puts pressure on a partnership.

Learning to understand your partner's feelings is the first step toward greater communication and a healthy relationship. However, it does not have to be difficult to improve your connection. To assist you, I've listed a few methods you can start to comprehend how your partner feels.

- **IT'S CRUCIAL TO PAY ATTENTION.**

Often, all people require is someone to listen to them. When your partner expresses their opinions, be fully present and let them speak.

- **SHOW THAT YOU CARE.**

Being present for your partner demonstrates that you care about them. When people want to convey their emotions, they usually only want someone to listen rather than try to solve the problem. Instead of giving advice, practice giving emotional support while they're talking, such as nods, supportive touches, or affirmative noises.

- **CONSIDER YOUR REACTION.**

Before you respond, make sure you fully get what your spouse says. You're not listening to your spouse if you're spending time planning a response to what they're saying while they're talking.

Before you start thinking about your response, wait for them to finish speaking and expressing themselves completely. Interjecting your thoughts into a moment your spouse expresses their feelings, you risk deterring them from truly opening up and revealing all.

Instead of being judgmental, try framing your response to encourage your spouse to continue talking. 'What do you think about that?' is an example of an open-ended question.

- **TAKE INTO ACCOUNT YOUR BODY LANGUAGE.**

Our facial expressions and body language frequently reveal more about our feelings than we realize. Body language may offer you a fair idea of your partner's present mood, so adjust your tone of voice and level of support accordingly.

When conversing with a partner, it's equally crucial to pay attention to your body language. If you are turned or facing away, you are not presenting yourself as someone open to debate.

When you mimic your partner, you indicate that you are receptive to chatting by keeping your arms uncrossed, comfortable posture, and making eye contact.

- **DO NOT BECOME ENRAGED.**

People often go on the defensive in relationships as an initial response to a partner expressing an idea or feeling they disagree with. You're telling your spouse that you think you're right and they're wrong by acting defensive. This may make your partner hesitant to open out to you or reveal their true feelings.

It's vital to remember that you don't have to agree on everything in a relationship. A quarrel is frequently the result of a misunderstanding, and allowing your spouse to speak without becoming unduly defensive may be all that is required.

- **RECOGNIZE YOUR FEELINGS.**

Internal obstacles can hamper our interactions. You're undoubtedly going through many ideas, sentiments, and emotions right now, which might make it difficult to understand what your partner is experiencing.

People frequently project their feelings onto their partners and think they feel the same way or refuse to accept that a spouse can have a different emotional reaction to a circumstance.

You will likely begin to recognize why you respond to things in specific ways and can detect how your partner reacts differently if you connect to your feelings and understand your emotional requirements.

- **FEEL FREE TO EXPRESS YOUR FEELINGS.**

We can inspire our partners to do the same by expressing our own emotions. You'll better understand each other's feelings if you openly talk and communicate your emotions.

- **STOP MAKING ASSUMPTIONS AND START COMMUNICATING.**

Asking your partner how they feel is sometimes the simplest thing to do. Some people believe that they should be able to comprehend their partner's emotions right away, yet this might lead to false conclusions. Instead, the best way to address it is to discuss it openly and honestly with your partner. Efficacious communication will help you create a stronger bond.

HOW TO BETTER UNDERSTAND YOUR PARTNER'S EMOTIONS: PRACTICAL ILLUSTRATION

Are you angered or hot while discussing emotions? Steps to take: Take a deep breath and consider it.

Making spouses express, listen to, and "understand" their feelings is key to repairing relationships. When I see John openly communicating his uncertainty and anger about being dismissed from his work and his partner Laura comprehending the felt sense of John's experience in that time, I recognize that John "feels felt,"—and Laura knows her empathy and understanding are correct.

Will John continue to be open about his emotions outside of his treatment sessions? Will Laura's empathy be as accurate as before? According to a recent study, the answer is a resounding and reassuring YES.

Researchers asked 155 mixed-sex couples to identify a persistent point of contention in their relationship. With the help of the participants, independent observers analyzed their recorded 11-minute dispute resolution sessions. Their purpose was to see if more emotional expressiveness on the part of the sharer was linked to more empathetic accuracy on the part of the perceiver.

According to the study's findings, any unambiguous statement of one partner's emotional experience improves the accuracy of the other partner's perception of that moment. In other words, it doesn't make sense to hide your feelings in couples counseling, but it does make sense to give emotional expression the attention it deserves.

This study demonstrates that the ability to be empathically accurate or fully "understand" another person's perspective may be transferred to other moments or situations. (This is fantastic news for John and Laura!)

According to this study, it doesn't matter whether you're expressing a well-thought-out thought or a spontaneous emotion; if the feeling is clear and the partner is paying attention and genuinely tuned in, the accuracy of the empathy seems to keep steady for both thoughts and feelings.

These findings may seem intuitive to you. Clear communication leads to clear comprehension. So, what prevents you from accurately assessing your partner's thoughts and feelings?

When one spouse detects a veiled criticism from the other, they usually react with surprise. The awareness of that startle response and continuing attention to any sensations or thoughts voiced keep the lines of communication open and the empathy correct.

Surprisingly, the researchers repeatedly found that perceptions of criticism in those thoughts and feelings did not affect empathic accuracy. (With the proviso, the conflict setting for the couples in the study was not particularly distressing, and thus participants may have been hesitant to report feeling threatened.)

Many adults haven't learned how to feel their feelings, let alone believe that someone else will be interested in hearing and caring about them. Many people have also not had enough practice listening to those closest to them without devaluation, defensiveness, or dispute.

The study's conclusion, which verifies a basic tenet of couples therapy, is that when one spouse expresses their thoughts and feelings more, the other partner may more properly infer their thoughts and feelings and subsequent moments throughout the relationship.

So, how do therapists today assist clients in learning these skills? To communicate themselves clearly and honestly at the moment and digest those communications with curiosity, open-mindedness, and accurate empathy?

THESE THREE STAGES HAVE PROVEN TO BE CRUCIAL IN MY EXPERIENCE.

1. Break it up into smaller pieces

Therapists assist clients in s-l-o-w-i-n-g d-o-w-n. One thought or sensation at a time, one bite-sized piece of information at a time.

"I feel so lost, not sure what to do next," John can say. Allow Laura time to hear and respond to what you've said. "I sense the disorientation, and I'm a little lost." "Are you able to elaborate?" The willingness to teach more drives people to share more.

Of course, there will likely be a slew of emotions and thoughts spinning around each other that need to be unpacked, named, and honored. Laura can inquire about the intricacies of John's anger as he says, "I'm feeling angry, too." "Of course, you'd be enraged. That's logical. I'd like to learn more about that to be confident I'm on the right track."

When his experience moves John, he can go deeper into his emotions: "I feel singled out." Laura will be able to stay with him while his emotions and thoughts change. "That appears to be essential. Tell me more about your experience of being singled out. I'd like to double-check that I understand."

Active Listening is a skill that allows you to pay attention. Empathy and understanding can help you connect with a partner.

Chunking stuff down encourages people to communicate more feelings and thoughts, ensuring that open communication and empathy are correct.

2. Take a breather

Couples can also learn to pause and double-check their empathy as they go. "This is what I said," John tells Laura. "Did you hear what I said?" "This is what I heard you say,"

Laura may tell John. Is that correct? "Did I understand correctly?"

This allows John to convey his feelings exactly as they are in the moment and Laura the opportunity to empathize with the true meaning fully.

The therapist might also use these questions to slow down the process: "John, this is what I heard you say." "Do I have that right?"

When couples are in a lot of dispute, pausing is necessary to keep the talk on track. Therapists may need to co-regulate the nervous system's reactivity in cases where the client's nervous system has gone into fight-flight-freeze-collapse survival mode, which can override the higher brain's ability to recognize and respond to our current feelings. Therapists may recommend softly caressing the heart with the hand, feeling the earth with the feet, deep breathing, or making eye contact with each other or the therapist. After a minute of being more present, the clients can resume checking in.: "This is what I said"; "This is what I heard."

But the most important thing for couples is to practice these abilities as often as possible when they are at home in their daily lives.

3. Think about it.

The chunking and pausing techniques provide both partners more time to analyze feelings and thoughts intentionally and reflect rather than react. " Aware of their feelings and thoughts, "I hadn't quite thought about it this way before." "Yes, I realize I'm sad when you talk about missing the camaraderie with your employees," the listener can say.

John feels affirmed when he learns that Laura hears him accurately (no editorializing, no remark). His story is true, and it matters. It matters because his partner insists on it, which strengthens their bond. Laura can remain open to the next communication from John, and the next, and the next, until she is satisfied that she is "getting it" from him. Even after many days, she may maintain her empathetic accuracy.

These three steps—chunk it down, pause, and reflect—create a sense of comfort in the couple that encourages honest, open conversation and allows them to regulate their emotions, which adds to the feeling of safety.

According to several theoretical perspectives, our sentiments either initiate or drive our thinking (narratives). Both points of view have value, and it's reassuring that the study's findings hold whether the sharing partner is sharing thoughts or feelings.

The core of any therapeutic process is making experience apparent. This can include bringing a client's current experience into explicit awareness so that they and their partner can be mindful and accepting of themselves and each other. If they can be with that experience, be interested in it, and even befriend it, empathy and compassion for each other will emerge. Helping clients do this independently enhances their connection's sense of safety, trust, and healing. This new research offers us a strong green light to do just that.

IS LOW EMOTIONAL INTELLIGENCE AFFECTING YOUR RELATIONSHIP?

People with low EQ, in general, are unable to understand their own and others' emotions effectively. They can be difficult to get along with on a personal and social level and difficult to work with because they cannot respond to even the most well-intentioned and constructive criticism. They are quick to blame, make excuses, and pass judgment on others, ultimately self-destructive, especially in relationships.

IS EMOTIONAL INTELLIGENCE SOMETHING WE'RE BORN WITH?

No, is the quick response. According to research, emotional intelligence is not something we are born with; rather, we gain it through experience. The foundations are built in our childhood, and our major caregivers, usually our parents, are crucial in instilling these talents in us. If you grew up in a loving environment with emotionally competent parents, you're likely to have gained these talents. If this was not the case, you might have battled to manage your emotions as a child, and forming deep relationships has been difficult. People don't seem to understand you, and you don't understand them.

WHAT CHARACTERISTICS DO PEOPLE WITH LOW EMOTIONAL INTELLIGENCE SHARE?

Many actions indicate a low EQ. This list is by no means complete, but it will give you an idea of the difficulties these people confront. As you read through each one, consider whether any of them ring true in your life and, if so, what you can do to change them.

1. **They don't form meaningful bonds with others.**

Consider someone you know who has trouble making friends. Is it possible that it's you? We can be certain that humans are genetically programmed to bond. We all require meaningful relationships to flourish, be happy, and live long, healthy lives. Mutual exchange of ideas, demonstrating empathy, being sympathetic, and offering support to those we care about, establishing strong and lasting ties.

However, when we lack crucial EQ skills, we go through life alone because it is difficult to create meaningful and lasting friendships.

We are not only uninformed of our own emotions and behaviors and how they affect others, but we are also unable to gauge the feelings of others and hence frequently 'put our foot in it.' We have the option to set things right if the buddy is brave enough to give us feedback. On the other hand, most friends will remain silent and 'drift' away from the friendship. As a result, we miss out on opportunities to form meaningful connections, leading to self-imposed isolation.

We may, however, change this habit by taking the time to get to know other people and fighting the need to talk more than we listen. People are more willing to offer additional details about their lives if they feel listened to. As a result, there is a chance to have a meaningful conversation and create trust in the relationship.

2. They aren't conscious of their existence.

I observed a road rage incident. Two drivers got out of their cars and started fighting in front of me. Like most other drivers delayed at the traffic lights, I was taken aback. My doors were reflexively locked. Neither man appeared to be conscious of their actions and, after an eternity, got back into their automobiles and drove away.

This is an example of a lack of emotional awareness and how our actions affect others. Furthermore, a lack of ability to self-regulate is a crucial symptom of low EQ. We sometimes can't identify our feelings or what's coming up for us because of low self-awareness, and as a result, we don't understand our behavior. Frustration, impatience, and rage are normal emotional outbursts, and we often react without thinking about what we're saying.

Emotionally intelligent people have a genuine and realistic grasp of themselves, their emotions, how they show up in life, and how they affect others.

3. **They are aware of their emotions, but they do not allow them to control their life.**

They respond to circumstances intellectually rather than emotionally. When they notice their sentiments becoming more intense, they hit the pause button to give themselves some breathing room and regain control of their emotions. When responding to any situation, they are mindfully present.

Self-awareness, compassion, and social intelligence can develop through genuine introspection and getting to know oneself.

Have you ever had a conversation with someone, and as soon as you start talking about your life, they take over and start talking about themselves? Maybe they have a better example or a more intriguing narrative to tell than you? Because persons with poor EQ can't comprehend or understand other people's emotions or the need to give them space to express themselves, they tend to focus on themselves in every discussion, circumstance, and situation. Whatever we're talking about, they always manage to find a way to bring the subject back to them. This is a surefire method to make the other person feel ignored and shut down.

4. **They not only direct the conversation to their realm, but they also tend to dominate it by asking rhetorical questions rather than open-ended ones.**

This query style is frequently used to catch or hold your attention while preventing you from hearing our response. We are also unable to react because of the nature of the question.

People with low EQ can't completely open up to be available to others, and they don't usually allow others to do so either. They are frequently emotional manipulators and calculating and dominating by nature. Instead of listening to talk, we can break this cycle by strengthening our active listening skills and allowing the other person to speak until they run out of things to say before offering our viewpoint, narrative, or point of view.

I can't help but think about my older brother when it comes to this. "I am never wrong," he once stated with a cheeky smile. I used to believe I was wrong, but I was wrong." Most of us know someone who has an opinion on everything and believes that theirs is the only valid viewpoint and that they cannot possibly be incorrect. If they are proved to be wrong, they find it difficult to apologize and confess their error. They frequently debate with others to persuade or agree with them. And if the other person fails to show up, they just dismiss them and their perspective as unimportant. They frequently lack sympathy, cannot sympathize with others, and are sometimes viewed as bullies.

This tendency can be disrupted by learning to recognize, hear, and feel other people's emotions and then shaping our responses and behaviors accordingly. Building trusting relationships requires accepting that we cannot always be correct and that other people may know more than we do.

5. They are never wrong.

Is this something you've heard before? Do you know someone who is never at fault, no matter the situation? A low exam score is due to the instructor's fault or a problem with the exam. When having a difficult conversation with a client, it is frequently the client's responsibility to fail to listen. Someone else in the team is to blame for a project missing a deadline.

People with poor EQ have a hard time accepting responsibility for anything. They are incapable of seeing mistakes as opportunities to learn and progress. Because they cannot admit a mistake, they will never be able to learn from it and will consequently be more likely to make mistakes. They'll most likely continue to blame the same scapegoat when that happens.

Even under the best of circumstances, receiving feedback is challenging. When we hear input, our primitive minds feel threatened and act protective. Being conscious of this natural tendency to feel defensive is a good place to start when dealing with critique. Seeing comments as an opportunity to learn something new, fill in a gap you weren't aware of, or try something new is priceless.

We can break the habit by acknowledging the error, determining our role, and identifying the lessons to be learned.

The first step in developing emotional intelligence is admitting that we lack it. The good news is that emotional intelligence can be taught and that we have complete control over our ability to do so. So, if you think your EQ could use some work, why not start right now? Perhaps you should risk asking a loved one if any of the behaviors above apply to you. Yes, I realize it will be a great risk, but take it nonetheless. Or perhaps you recognize your floors and realize that this is an area on which you need to spend more time.

Most of us desire to have happy and resourceful partnerships throughout our lives. Healthy connections are also essential for our mental and emotional well-being.

HOW TO DEAL WITH A RELATIONSHIP WITH LOW EMOTIONAL INTELLIGENCE

When we consider what we want in a spouse, we may have a list of qualities in mind. Their physical appearance, sense of humor, hobbies, interests, or ethics could be factors. However, we frequently overlook one of the most important factors contributing to a happy relationship: emotional intelligence.

A healthy and happy relationship requires a high level of emotional intelligence. High levels of emotional intelligence have been demonstrated to boost marital satisfaction in research. So, how can you determine if someone lacks emotional intelligence, and what can you do to improve your compatibility?

Emotional intelligence is concerned with your ability to recognize and control your emotions so that you can express them appropriately. It becomes easier to build interpersonal interactions and strengthen good attributes like empathy and sympathy.

Emotional intelligence facilitates communication. Communication is essential in a successful relationship, and if you're dating someone with poor emotional intelligence, it may feel like you're dating an immature and sullen teenager! There are so many deep feelings in a relationship that having a high level of emotional intelligence is almost essential if you wish to successfully communicate and comprehend your spouse.

So, if you're having trouble communicating successfully with your partner, might it be due to a lack of emotional intelligence? Here are some of the telltale indications of emotional intelligence deficiency.

THERE ARE FIVE FREQUENT INDICATORS OF LOW EMOTIONAL INTELLIGENCE.

1. **What is the benefit to them?**

At first glance, your companion appears to be giving, kind, and nice to others. These appear to be excellent indications, and they are qualities you desire in a partner. Is it true that they are simply being polite because it benefits them? They may, for example, donate to a charity to gain respect, recognition, and attention for their acts. They may tip the waiter excessively to receive better treatment the next time. If it's evident that they're simply doing nice things because they get something in return, they might not be very giving.

If it appears that your partner is merely doing something to benefit themselves, this is a sign of inadequate emotional intelligence. Pay attention to your instincts; if their behavior appears to be fake or extreme, it most likely is.

2. The focal point of attention

We've all encountered that person who has had it worse and for longer than you. Perhaps you've tried to chat about your life, but the topic always returns to them? People will occasionally ask inquiries that appear to be of interest. This may lead you to feel they possess a high level of emotional intelligence. However, in most cases, the other person will have the ultimate word on the subject or steer the conversation to their own experiences.

3. Commitment-phobe

If you're often getting let down at the last minute, it's another clue that the individual who's flaking on you lacks emotional intelligence. They don't have a high level of emotional knowledge if they can't be honest or understand their boundaries enough to decline an invitation in advance. Furthermore, this individual will lack the empathy to respect your time and schedule by informing you ahead of time.

4. Hypocritical critic

Another symptom of low emotional intelligence is when someone constantly criticizes and discusses other people's problems while failing to see their own. Those with a high level of emotional intelligence will be able to recognize their strengths and flaws. Furthermore, they will empathize with them rather than blame or criticize people.

People who have little emotional intelligence will criticize others for justifying their actions. "The project fell short of expectations not because of my work, but because I was given bad information and my colleague doesn't know how to prepare reports correctly," for example.

"You know how anxious I get when you do X and Y," or "You know how agitated I get when you do X and Y." I'm offended that you're so insensitive when you know how upset you make me and still do X and Y."

consider the following:

It can be helpful to have someone present to point you on the right path in some situations. A person who gives continuous and dismissive counsel, on the other hand, can be extremely destructive and damaging in some instances. If you can't express a concern or talk about your life without someone advising you on what to do or providing their opinion on the subject, you may have low emotional intelligence.

Instead, someone with great emotional intelligence will try to comprehend your feelings. They'll also try to figure out whether you're searching for advice, support, or just a safe place to vent.

5. Dealing with a lack of emotional intelligence

It's crucial to remember that emotional intelligence isn't a skill that everyone possesses. People may be unable to be attentive, empathic, or in sync with others. There are, however, ways to express your emotions and increase communication with someone who isn't emotionally intelligent.

MANAGING YOUR EMOTIONS IN A RELATIONSHIP

A buddy told me that he was finding it increasingly difficult to manage his wife's emotions, which had been more ups and downs than a rollercoaster. He'd freeze like a deer in headlights when she became upset, whether it was about him, the kids, or some other force she expected him to be aware of and empathize with. Unfortunately, he'd accuse her of being overly sensitive because he didn't understand the situation, and she'd storm out of the room.

This is easier said than done because men and women deal with emotions and sentiments differently. Instead of focusing on our differences, we should concentrate on managing our own emotions and accepting our partners. In addition, we must exercise extreme caution in our acts and conduct.

Unfortunately, emotional detachment and not being able to meet our spouse's demands is a common tendency that leads to estrangement or worse. Long, happy marriages require emotional connection and the ability to handle emotions in a partnership.

WHAT ARE EMOTIONS, AND HOW DO THEY AFFECT US?

Feelings are referred to as emotions. To begin to comprehend your feelings, you must first ask yourself two questions: Others, on the other hand, have feelings. You must be conscious of your sentiments while also being aware of the feelings of others.

We can discern how others feel in various ways, but one of the most effective is monitoring what they say and how they behave, including their body language. According to studies, more than 80% of communication is nonverbal, which is communicated through body language and facial expression. Because many of us dislike talking about our feelings, especially when they are strong, we tend to convey them more through our body language.

Emotions are not something that can be intentionally controlled. The limbic system is the region of the brain that deals with emotions. This portion of the brain is thought to have evolved rather early in human history, making it quite primitive. This explains why an emotional response is frequently simple but extremely powerful: you want to cry, flee, or scream.

It's because these responses are motivated by a desire to survive.

Emotions and memories are inextricably linked. If you've had a poor experience before, your emotional reaction to the same stimulus will likely be intense.

Babies are capable of feeling emotion but not necessarily reasoning. Emotions and values are inextricably linked: an emotional response could indicate that one of your core principles has been questioned.

Understanding the connection between memories and values is crucial to controlling your emotional reaction. Your emotional responses may or may not be related to the current situation or logic, but you can overcome them by using logic and being aware of your feelings.

Take some time to pay attention to your emotional responses and explore what might be causing them, such as values, memories, or experiences.

Consider what causes pleasant emotions and what causes negative ones.

Remember that you have the power to change your feelings. You can perform well when you have a lot of positive energy, but you can't stay in that state forever. You'll have to minimize your energy consumption sooner or later. Maintain a cheerful attitude, and you will swiftly heal. You'll burn out if you indulge in more unpleasant emotions.

HOW CAN WE CONTROL OUR EMOTIONS IN A RELATIONSHIP EFFECTIVELY?

1. **Refrain from negative energy** - all emotions are normal and healthy.

On the other hand, emotions and behaviors are two completely distinct things, and it's the unmanaged behaviors that lead to a breakdown in communication or unmet needs. This can involve being defensive, yelling, making gestures like an eye roll, or leaving the room out of irritation. The best way to manage emotions and conflict is to have positive emotional dialogue and create a safe environment.

2. Ask your spouse if he or she is okay

We may not realize what we did wrong or what provoked our spouse's emotional outburst at first. And that's perfectly fine. Rather than dismissing it as hypersensitivity, inquire whether they are okay or what is bothering them. You've created a nice environment for your spouse to voice their grievances. And once they've vented their frustrations, you can collaborate to find a solution.

3. Share your sentiments

Building on the previous point, you may effectively manage emotions in a relationship by ensuring that your feelings are properly communicated. As a result, strong back-and-forth communication should emerge, allowing the difficulties to be resolved quickly.

Don't add to the drama by pointing fingers or accusing your spouse; instead, express your thoughts and feelings. It is far more beneficial to state how you feel and why you feel that way.

4. **Don't expect to solve everything in one night – managing emotions in a relationship may necessitate multiple conversations.**

This is especially true if the first one or two occur when one or both of you are irritated. Both of you must feel comfortable revisiting the subject. But don't wait too long. When one or both of you are ready, talk about it.

IT'S CRITICAL TO UNDERSTAND EMOTIONS IN YOUR RELATIONSHIP

Conflicts inevitably arise, and the trick is to avoid being provoked. In a relationship, we all go through millions of emotions, and those feelings produce brain chemicals that modify how we feel. Sometimes (preferably most of the time), we are in a happy state of mind, and other times we are neutral or even have bad feelings about our relationships and ourselves.

Part of having a great relationship is being able to trust your partner with your emotions. When you discuss something personal with your partner, such as a worry about something at work, and they are supportive, trust is built. It also offers you additional stamina to deal with whatever problem you're dealing with.

On the other hand, if your partner puts you down or is unsupportive, you may be less open about how you're feeling now and in the future. This unhealthy dynamic must be handled to avoid damage or conflict in any relationship.

When conflicts arise, take a look at how you communicate with one another. Certain words can set off a chain reaction, so you should be cautious about saying anything that could be disrespectful or lead you to respond adversely or shut down. If you know, certain words or phrases would irritate your partner and cause a disagreement, avoid using them and instead learn to talk from your heart rather than your anger.

It's tough to trust others when you're sad or furious, and it's even harder to trust someone angry with you. Suppose you don't find a method to be pleasant to each other again after experiencing emotional disturbance frequently. In that case, your relationship will be unable to progress and will slowly decline. Deciding to be kinder to the person with whom you share your life can be as simple as committing to doing so. I promise it will make a difference if you say your pledge out loud—and when you do, please look in each other's eyes and feel your connection.

One method to keep this new commitment is to treat your partner better than everyone else in your life, even other family members. This is not to mean that you treat others badly, but you should make an effort to make your partner feel special on occasion. That's all it takes, and if you do it every day, your love will grow a little bit. It's a wonderful habit to form together, and it will only strengthen your bond.

Recognize when your partner does something you find appealing, attractive, or exceptional as another strategy for increasing intimacy. Validating your partner will help build your relationship and bring you closer together. We can't relate in a vacuum, and both of you need to show how much you care if you want to generate the happiness you both deserve.

HOW TO TAKE CONTROL OF YOUR EMOTIONS

Emotional overreactions affect us all. We say something to someone we care about without thinking about the repercussions in the heat of the moment. Or we send an email and then wonder why we didn't think about it before sending it. Our emotions overflow and the damage is done by the time they subside.

In the public sphere, hardly a day goes by without a newspaper front-page story about a controversy sparked by comments, tweets, or emails. After that, the next story begins.

In the opposite scenario, we are overwhelmed by dread or worry and fail to grab the opportunity to speak up or act following our principles. The repercussions of freezing can be just as bad, if not worse, than those of overreacting. In any case, controlling our emotions is a difficult task.

When we reflect on these events, we frequently say, "My emotions got the best of me." But this presents a crucial question: do I control my emotions, or do they control me? Nobody at school asked me this question or told me the answer. As a result, I entered adulthood with a royal flush of emotions ranging from delight and excitement to fear and rage and no instruction on managing them.

The truth is that in this area, we've ended up with a tangled mess of counsel. Much of the conventional wisdom advises us to suppress negative emotions and replace them with good ones. According to other experts, this is akin to putting the icing on dog food and calling it cake. So, if someone is correct, who is it?

To go through this emotional minefield, we need to make a few key distinctions:

We can't switch emotions on and off like a faucet. Whether we like it or not, they will come and go. You may stop expecting undesirable emotions to go gone once you understand this. The notion that we can expel them is unhelpful and unconvincing. They are an inextricable element of the human experience. Furthermore, the more we seek to conduct our lives following our ideals and convictions, the more our emotions will rise to confront us.

Emotions are neither good nor bad. The human brain is hardwired to classify things as positive or negative, especially sensitive to dangers. This made evolutionary sense for our forefathers, who had to learn to react to external threats to survive. We applied the same classification technique to our internal state, including our emotions, as humans produced language. As a result, we see joy as positive and welcome, while fear is negative and undesirable.

This, however, poses other issues. According to the principle that 'what we oppose persists,' ignoring negative emotions simply strengthens their grip. So, what's the other option? It can be extremely freeing to feel the whole gamut of human emotions without assigning positive or negative labels to them. Take, for example, Dame Judi Dench, who has won one Oscar, two Golden Globes, and ten BAFTA awards. According to her, the more she acts, the more terrified she feels. Thousands of aspiring performers wait for the day when they'll be able to overcome their fear, but she treats it as a friend rather than an enemy. This is not to suggest that she is at ease with her fear, but she makes no attempt to overcome it, so it does not define her. "I'm afraid," she admits. "I'd be lost without it." Maybe that's why her on-screen characters are so human.

You aren't your feelings.

Emotions are powerful by their sheer nature. It's critical to understand that you are not your feelings. You are a person with strong ideals and commitments who experiences emotions on a frequent and ongoing basis. This point may appear to be semantic, but it is not. When we get fused, we are essentially hijacked by our emotions, believing that 'they' and 'we' are the same thing. Emotions no longer control your behavior if you can notice them without becoming them.

We always have the option to choose. A single thought or emotion does not preclude you from taking action. It's simple to believe that "I'm afraid and can't speak," but this is a mental trick. "I'm afraid, and choosing not to speak" would be more realistic and authentic. The ability to examine our emotions, even when they feel overwhelming, creates a place where we can relate to our commitments and ideals. While we may not always be able to control our emotions, we can control how we react to them. This is where accountability comes in, and responsibility is arguably the closest thing humans have to a superpower.

EMOTIONAL INTELLIGENCE AND MANAGING RELATIONSHIPS

Emotional intelligence can considerably enhance people's ability to lead and manage their relationships. Evidence demonstrates that those with higher emotional intelligence have more successful careers and relationships than people with lower levels.

EMOTIONAL INTELLIGENCE AND RELATIONSHIP MANAGEMENT

Relationship management refers to a collection of abilities engaged in creating relationships with others in the context of emotional intelligence. Consider the following 17 relationship management and emotional intelligence strategies:

1. **Be open and interested.**

Give a brief history of yourself and some personal details. When you willingly divulge details about yourself, you reduce the chances that others may misinterpret your actions.

2. **Make yourself available.**

People must feel at ease when approaching you. Adopt an "open-door" policy to accomplish this. This lets coworkers come in and have impromptu chats about concerns, projects, or seeking advice.

3. **Embrace feedback.**

Having someone point out flaws or areas for growth might elicit strong emotions. You can feel like you've been called out or put on the spot. On the other hand, feedback is critical to the growth and requires that you hear it without allowing your emotions to get in the way. To improve your ability to take feedback, do the following:

4. **Develop trust**

It's tough to gain trust, but it's easy to lose it. To form ties with those around you, use patience and stick to what you say you're doing. To start creating trust, do the following:

5. **Work on your communication skills.**

How others view you is determined by your natural communication style. Others may not comprehend what you're trying to express if the way you speak does not match your goals, and they may develop negative feelings toward you. To have a better understanding of how you communicate and how you may enhance it

6. **Avoid sending mixed messages with**

They perplex and irritate people. When talking, make sure your tone of voice and body language sync with what you attempt to express. If you tell an employee that you're excited to have them on a project, but you do so with slumped shoulders and a disengaged tone, they will not believe you.

Even persons with high emotional intelligence have their emotions come to the surface. Relationship management does not include concealing or suppressing emotions; rather, it entails properly and constructively expressing them.

When you're overwhelmed by negative feelings, try to put them away until you have a chance to express them fully and in a setting where they won't be harmful. You'll have to get through your emotions eventually, but if you let them get in the way of the message you're trying to communicate, you'll send mixed signals. Be honest if you can't put your feelings aside. Describe what's going on and how you're feeling.

7. **Explain your decisions.**

People are afraid of what they don't comprehend. If you keep others in the dark, they may become frustrated and anxious since they don't understand why you made a decision. When expressing your choices, identify alternatives, demonstrate your thought process, and explain how your choices affect everyone.

8. Make sure your impact matches your aim.

Your good intentions may backfire if you make inappropriate comments or fail to notice your coworkers' emotional states. Respect the feelings of others around you and think things through before acting.

9. Be aware of other people's feelings.

They won't respond well if you try to reject or ignore what they're feeling. Use your listening skills, inquire about what you can do to assist, and show empathy. This validates the other person's feelings without increasing or aggravating their emotional state.

10. Use basic courtesy

"Please," "thank you," and "I'm sorry" are all appropriate phrases to use. These phrases will help you boost morale and connect with your coworkers through reciprocal respect and admiration. These may appear insignificant, yet they serve as continual reminders to be considerate of those around you.

11. Express your gratitude.

Small gestures of gratitude can go a long way. Praise someone who accomplishes an excellent job. Recognize them when they go above and beyond. Small gestures, even if they're as simple as buying someone lunch or leaving a thank you letter, let the people around you know that you notice and appreciate what they're doing.

12. Only use rage on purpose.

When you express rage as an emotional response, you may appear out of control. When used as a tactic, though, it can effectively deliver a message. Only utilize your anger as a strategy if you believe you have a firm grasp on your emotions:

13. React correctly.

Read the situation, keep an eye out for signs that the person speaking to you is emotional, and answer in a way that respects their feelings. This enables you to assist others while maintaining their calm and rationality properly. Don't always mirror the emotions of the other person. This will worsen the tone of the conversation, especially in high-stress settings.

14. **Use "fix-it" sentences.**

When things grow heated, avoid pointing fingers and instead concentrate on resolving the issue. Fix-it statements are neutral statements that concentrate everyone's attention on the current situation. These can be direct remedies to the problem or acknowledgments like "this is difficult." They help to relieve tension and keep things from becoming too personal.

15. **Don't put off what you can't avoid.**

Unavoidable situations emerge from time to time that you aren't fully comfortable with. You may be required to work on a project that you dislike or with a teammate. Develop techniques to tackle your task productively while keeping your emotions in check in these instances.

When dealing with another person, be courteous yet direct. You don't have to tell them you despise them, but you need to figure out a way to collaborate without being too hostile. Use your EQ skills to adjust to the person, even by holding your tongue slightly.

16. Giving effective feedback.

Effective feedback necessitates applying all four EQ skills and demonstrates the EQ evolution.

Self-awareness: How do you feel about having to give feedback? Take note of your emotional reactions to the material you're presenting. If you're feeling uneasy or worried, attempt to determine why you feel that way.

Self-control: When giving feedback, keep your emotions in check regardless of your feelings. Create methods to keep yourself calm and on task using the information you gained from your self-awareness.

Consider how this input might affect the individual in front of you once you've grasped your own emotions. Please take into account their personality as well as their current emotional state.

Relationship management: Emotional intelligence entails functioning in a considerate manner of others' feelings. So, consider the most effective manner to convey feedback to the other person without discouraging or infuriating them.

17. Effectively manage challenging conversations

Maintain your composure, express empathy, and talk clearly:

Emotional intelligence requires the ability to handle relationships. It requires practice and perseverance to become proficient at it, just like any other talent. Keep going, and you'll improve day by day.

You can use relationship management to connect with others to make them feel understood and supported. Managing relationships is a crucial emotional intelligence talent that allows you to lead change or handle personal transformation effectively.

EMOTIONAL INTELLIGENCE: MAKING LOVE LAST

It takes commitment to be a life partner. Almost everyone would agree that trust and commitment are required for any successful relationship to thrive. But what are some of the other qualities that make a relationship mutually happy and loving?

People who are in relationships or want to find long-term love may ask what makes love last. What makes certain marriages or unions last and thrive while others fall apart? Emotionally savvy couples appear to be on to something. But what are they doing particularly to strengthen and grow their bonds?

"Without passion, there can be no knowledge." We may be conscious of the truth, but it is not ours until we have felt its force. The soul's experience must be added to the brain's cognition." — Author Enoch Arnold Bennet (Quoted in Goleman & Cherniss, 2001)

Emotional intelligence is crucial in relationships because emotions are the foundation upon which we build personal connections. Emotional intelligence includes a person's aptitude for empathy and their ability to talk about emotions in a healthy and caring manner. Emotional intelligence can be evident in many areas of a relationship or marriage. It is essential for making love last throughout a lifetime.

WHAT EXACTLY IS LOVE?

The word "love" can evoke various emotions and thoughts. These concepts may differ from one individual to the next. So, what exactly does love entail?

The English language can be fairly restrictive in its definition when it comes to studying love. Ancient Greek provides a much more comprehensive grasp of love's numerous facets. There are numerous distinct words for love in Ancient Greek: éros, philia, storg. Etc.

ESSENTIAL AREAS WHERE EMOTIONALLY INTELLIGENT COUPLES PRACTICE LOVE WELL

1. Friendship is at the heart of any successful relationship. Because they are friends who support and care for one other, emotionally intelligent couples stand the test of time. They have a strong relationship of affection. They are aware of each other's inner lives and each other's likes and dislikes. They are confidants and companions.

2. Emotionally intelligent couples have great feelings of admiration and respect for one another. They are capable of respecting and valuing their spouse and their wants and preferences. Partners usually think well of one other and appreciate each other's distinctive qualities, accomplishments, or abilities. They show their appreciation for one another daily, both verbally and nonverbally.

3. Couples who can communicate their thoughts, wants, and feeling healthy are more likely to have a successful relationship than those who struggle with

communication. They don't usually show symptoms of criticism or scorn in their interactions, and they don't start abruptly. Emotionally intelligent couples communicate with one another in a respectful manner, using tone, intonation, and intent to show this respect.

During his studies on couples, Dr. John Gottman discovered that conversations that start off brutally usually end badly. In fact, the first three minutes of a discussion are frequently decisive.

4. Couples that have strong, long-lasting relationships know how to deal with conflict. They've figured out how to deal with their differences and arguments. It isn't always true that they have fewer conflicts than other couples. Rather, they've figured out how to listen and comprehend the other's point of view or viewpoint. They've probably also figured out how to compromise in their relationship.

5. **Strengthening the bond between you and your partner:** Emotionally intelligent couples foster their connection by knowing their shared identity as a couple and their identities. They are confident in their jobs and the collaboration as a whole. They're for the sake of the connection. They don't threaten it with phrases like "I want a divorce" or "I'm leaving you." Instead, they discuss issues that develop as they happen. They seek professional assistance if the difficulties are too complex to solve independently.

6. **Setting and enforcing appropriate boundaries:** Couples who prosper set firm limits, especially when dealing with other people. They are aware of the dangers of infidelity and do not allow emotional or physical affairs to occur. They see the world through a glass window of transparency and honesty, whether they realize it. Together, they build a barrier that protects them from influences that could separate them or jeopardize their connection. They maintain a united face to keep their relationship a priority.

7. **Understanding the significance, worth, and purpose of one's life:** Couples who are emotionally savvy are aware of what is important to each other. This could be figuring out what drives the other person in life and what they care about, such as their hopes, objectives, or values. Couples who thrive encourage each other in their individual and joint efforts to live a meaningful and purposeful life.

8. **Couples who are happy together share their lives.** They make it a point to connect regularly. They are conscious of staying connected and leaning toward their spouse, whether they realize it. They share a few mutual interests or pastimes, and they spend time together relaxing and unwinding. "There is no antidote for love but to love more" (Henry David Thoreau)

It takes focus and devotion to make love last, but it is achievable. Being aware of how to practice éros, philia, and

storg love will assist you in making love last in many ?
of your life.

Recognition of one's own and others' emotions' is how emotional intelligence is defined. It's the ability to control and manage these feelings.' The key core dimensions of emotional intelligence are strongly aligned with an examination of emotional intelligence.

THE SIGNIFICANCE OF SELF-AWARENESS

Knowing and comprehending our feelings and strengthening our ability to deal with them is what self-awareness is all about. When we're in a relationship, we ask ourselves many questions. Did I, for example, discipline my child properly? Is it feasible for me to accept that my partner is motivated by their career and spends far too much time at work? Is it fair for my partner to spend more time on the golf course than at home? Is it possible that my relationship is about to end?

Self-awareness is a straightforward procedure. Understanding how you react to situations is crucial in accepting how you handle situations at home. On the other hand, limited awareness will result in distractions, disagreements, and possibly a connection deterioration. As a result, having a clear awareness of the situation and the ability to communicate it can lead to improved relationships.

Self-reflection can help you become more self-aware. Through reflection, people can better understand their own emotions and the repercussions of their actions on their partners. In other words, greater self-awareness leads to a better balance of family, career, and social life.

THE IMPORTANCE OF SELF-REGULATION

Understanding how your body reacts to emotions is central to the concept of self-regulation. Emotions are classified as either positive or negative. Positive emotions give people affirmations that help them find their way and focus. People who have good emotions are often happier and have a more balanced mental state. Negative emotions cause feelings of despair, worry, anxiety, and even depression in the body. These problems result in a loss of control.

As a result, people should try to control their emotions and recognize their own and others' feelings. As relationships swing back and forth between happiness and despair, controlling your emotions is crucial. Controlling one's emotions helps to create better mental processes. Supporting your spouse through postnatal depression, losing a loved one, or moving house, for example, can all lead to emotional upheaval.

Understanding your attitude will help you recognize your emotions and overcome unpleasant ones. For example, determine how you feel in situations that inspire positive and negative emotions. Accepting and discussing sentiments with loved ones is a good way to deal with them. Music or exercise may help you stay positive.

THE SIGNIFICANCE OF MOTIVATION

Motivation is a natural drive that benefits all aspects of human life. Human life could be almost non-existent without motivation. Maintaining motivation is beneficial and can aid in the development of relationships. Planning outings with the family to engage them will improve contentment.

Working with a partner might be a great way to boost your motivation. Having a weekly strategy is a great approach to staying on top of what's coming up.

Plans include going to the gym, seeing a movie, or visiting a garden center.

While it is understandable that work and exhaustion can interfere with family life, it is also essential that the core of family values be preserved. Doing things together can boost motivation and strengthen and value relationships.

THE IMPORTANCE OF EMPATHY

When it comes to helping one another, empathy is crucial. Being unable to empathize with a loved one can be harmful and should be addressed. Empathy is the ability to comprehend and appreciate needs, desires, and feelings. It would be beneficial to recognize partner needs and look into ways to address them to create empathy. We must consider whether we comprehend the needs of others. Are we capable of thinking or acting in the same way others do? We should try not to become overly focused on' but rather think of 'us.'

Having conversations about ways to help one another fosters empathy and desire.

Understanding oneself and others is the goal of emotional intelligence. We have a better chance of having good relationships if we practice self-awareness and develop techniques to help each other.

EMOTIONAL INTELLIGENCE IN LOVE AND INTIMATE RELATIONSHIP

Emotional intelligence (EQ) is the key to long-term intimate relationships, partly because it makes us acutely aware of the changes that occur in ourselves and others daily. If you improve your EQ, you'll have the sensitivity that each of us is looking for in a significant other. Through active awareness and empathy, you'll be able to detect small variations in your romance's dynamics that indicate a need for action.

Because of empathy, our intrinsic ability to share emotional experiences, we have the opportunity to achieve the kind of love we all desire—deep connection, reciprocal compassion, real commitment, soulful caring. To reach the pinnacle of romance, however, we'll need all of the skills of a high EQ: sharp emotional awareness to avoid mistaking infatuation or lust for lasting love; acceptance to experience emotions that could harm a relationship if left to fester; and a vigilant active awareness to assess what's working and what isn't.

CREATING EMOTIONALLY SAVVY ROMANTIC CONNECTIONS

We don't have to accept dullness or bickering in our romantic relationships. We don't have to pick the wrong lovers, wind up in several disastrous marriages, or allow our long-term relationships to lose their romance. We don't have to let opposing needs and desires stand in the way of two people in love.

Because of empathy and our intrinsic ability to share emotional experiences, we have the opportunity to achieve the kind of love we all desire—deep connection and mutual compassion, really dedicated, soulful caring. But, to achieve those relationship goals, we'll need all of the skills that come with a high EQ: astute emotional awareness to avoid mistaking infatuation or lust for lasting love, acceptance to experience emotions that can harm a relationship if left to rot, and vigilant active awareness to keep us informed about what's working and what isn't. Fortunately, your EQ doesn't have to be at its highest before you start dating. In reality, for many people, falling in love catalyzes heart reeducation. This is why some of the most ardent lovers are in their eighties: They realize that having two high EQs results in a romance that never stops growing, never loses its luster, and always strengthens them both individually and collectively.

Make a conscious effort to transform your relationship.

When you overcome your fear of change, you'll realize that different isn't always bad. On the other side of change, things frequently turn out better than before. Relationships are organisms in and of themselves, and they must alter to survive. Any connections that aren't moved toward the kind of change you desire may drift into a different form of change—perhaps one you don't want. Your courage and optimism are rewarded by your ability to welcome change. Is your partner in need of something new from you? Do you need to set aside some time to reevaluate your situation together? Is it necessary for you to change your duties due to external pressures? Are you as content as you once were? Such questions are frequently too frightening to tackle without EQ, so many partners disregard signs of change until it's too late.

Consider the difficulties you face as opportunities rather than problems.

Your courage and optimism enable you to see issues as challenging possibilities rather than problems. How inventive are you and your partner? When you don't have to blame each other for your feelings, you're less likely to be controlled by negative emotional memories, and you're more likely to avoid making the same mistake again. You can break free from ruts and resignation when you have a high EQ and get down to resourceful problem-solving. Differences between you and unavoidable disasters can be met as invitations to connect, challenges to get closer and emerge stronger individually and collectively.

All of your sentiments for each other should be respected.

We may not always be ecstatic with the new information we learn about the person we love, but we must accept them all when it comes to feelings. Being in love does not imply that you will never be angry, dissatisfied, upset, or jealous of your partner. It's up to you how you react to your feelings; what matters is that you feel them. Blame has damaged many marriages, and guilt has prevented millions of couples from experiencing genuine intimacy. Both are heinous remnants of unspoken rage, fear, and worry. If you've put in the effort to raise your EQ, you'll be able to feel the feelings and go on with your life.

Maintain a sense of humor in your relationship.

You need acceptance to avoid intellectualizing emotions, and laughter is a significant acceptance component. Couples who can't laugh at themselves aren't likely to be very accepting of their relationships. They might not be able to put up with its shortcomings and inevitable stumbles any longer than they can with their own. They're also less likely to be open to the most delightful surprises in a relationship. On the other hand, your high EQ means you can continue to improve your relationship while never succumbing to intolerant expectations of perfection.

Take note of how you feel when your lover isn't present.

Fortunately, you have a foolproof method of keeping track of how your relationship progresses: To figure out how the rest of your life is going, use the three well-being indicators. Do you have general restlessness or irritability? Do you dread going to work or school the next day after a night of marital bliss? Do you despise your family and friends, even though you spend every available minute alone with them? Tunnel vision is never a good thing when it comes to love. It doesn't matter if you coo like doves when you're together if you don't feel energetic, clear-headed, and generous all of the time. Something isn't right if the sex is perfect, but you're struggling at work, if you feel comfortable and secure hearing "Hi, honey" when you arrive home at night but can't get out of bed in the morning, even if everything is warm and fuzzy in the castle.

When this happens, all of the information your emotions and intellect have accumulated about you, your lover, and your relationship will guide you to the optimal answer.

Identifying "the one."

How can you determine if this person is "the one" when you initially fall in love? How can you tell if you're in love with a genuine person or merely with love? How do you avoid repeating your mistakes if you've already been burned?

Pay attention to your body rather than your mind.

We choose a partner for reasons that have less to do with how we feel and more to do with how we think. We conduct our interactions in the manner they should or have been conducted. This is precisely where we go astray. We don't lose love because we let our emotions control us; we lose love because we let our heads control us.

For a variety of reasons, people believe they are in love: lust, infatuation, a desire for stability, status, or social acceptability. They believe they've met genuine love since the current prospect matches a stereotype or expectation. However, until individuals know their feelings, their decision is doomed to fail. Breathe, relax, and focus on getting out of your head and checking in with your body if your daydreams of a potential lover take the shape of mental dialogues rationalizing or agonizing over your decision. If you have a persistent or growing sense that something is wrong, your decision is most likely incorrect. You'll never know what you want if you let mental images rather than physical sensations guide you.

Pay attention to your full body's messages.

Most individuals find it difficult to obtain clear messages from their entire body during new love since sexual desire typically drowns them out, so it's crucial to pay attention to other, more subtle impulses. Muscle tension, migraines, stomach problems, and a lack of energy are signs that what you want isn't always what you need. If the glow of love is accompanied by an increase in vitality and liveliness, on the other hand, this could be the real deal. If it's more than passion or infatuation, you'll notice a difference in other areas of your life and relationships. Consider the following high-EQ questions:

Is this relationship invigorating my entire life? Has my work, for example, improved? Is it true that I'm taking better care of myself? Is it possible for me to stand up straighter? Is it true that I'm more focused, creative, and responsible? Do my "in love" feelings extend beyond a nice feeling of caring for my partner? Do I feel more kind, giving, and empathic with friends, coworkers, or complete strangers? If the answers you get from your body aren't what you're looking for, attempt to push over your natural fear of loss. Knowing that you haven't discovered real love can save you the agony of a lifetime of poor emotional memories—a legacy that keeps you repeating the same mistakes or turns you off to love entirely.

Take a chance and reach out to someone.

When we meet someone new, we're naturally wary and put up barriers to getting to know them. It's scary to leave yourself open and vulnerable at this point, but it's the only way to find out if true love is feasible between you and if you're both falling for the same person or a ruse. Try being the first to reach out—share a personal secret, laugh at yourself, or express affection when it's the most difficult. Does their response make you feel warm and alive? If that's the case, you might have found a kindred spirit. If not, you may have encountered someone with a poor EQ and must decide how to respond.

Responding to a romantic partner with a low EQ

Emotional muscle does not grow at the same rate for everyone. Here are some high-EQ methods to respond to low-EQ conduct and bad listeners if you're ahead of the one you love.

Take some time to think about your sentiments and the words you want your spouse to hear. Your message may be muddled if you're unclear on what you need and why you need it. Choose a time when neither you nor your spouse is rushed or irritated. Take a walk together or plan a brunch or dinner date, but keep the booze to a minimum if you want them to remember the conversation. If you want your partner to know something is wrong with them, send "I feel" messages regarding your needs. "For example, I'd like to make love more regularly, but I'm allergic to onions and garlic odors, so would you mind brushing your teeth before bed?" If your partner becomes defensive in response to your feelings, state their concerns again: "You're scared that you and the kids will be neglected if I take this job." Repeat your "I feel" message, then listen again until you're certain you've been heard.

IF YOU'RE NEW TO LOVE OR EQ, THESE POINTERS WILL HELP YOU STAY ON TRACK:

You're in a relationship with a future if you feel invigorated, cognitively clear, and more loving. Make your feelings known to your partner. If you're going to say anything, say what you think because it defines who you are. You'll never feel appreciated if you pretend to be someone or something you're not. Listen with your emotions in mind. As you listen to your lover's words, pay attention to their feelings. Show your love and support for your partner. A suggestion or a helping hand may be useful or reassuring to one person, but it may be bothersome. Not everyone appreciates being touched in the same way, being affectionate in public, or receiving gifts in the same way. Allow empathy to lead you. If you're unsure, ask. You don't get to know everything because you're in love. You'll never know how your sweetheart feels about anything unless you ask. Prepare to put effort into the relationship. Why do so many individuals assume that their work is done once they've found true love?

Relationships can either develop and grow with attention or wither and perish if they are neglected. Take advice from your partner. Active awareness prevents you from making assumptions based on previous experiences. Keep an eye out for any emotional memories. The emotional repercussions of previous wrongdoings are the most hazardous to those we care about today. Keep in mind that the only issue with making mistakes is not admitting them. Because of the intricacy of relationships, mistakes are inevitable, but they may also be opportunities for progress if handled without blame. Change should be viewed as a chance to strengthen your relationship. Any change is unpleasant, but it also allows your relationship to be renewed and revitalized.

WHAT YOU REQUIRE TO FEEL LOVED VS. WHAT YOU DESIRE

Know the difference between what you can't live without and what you'd want to locate the person who is truly "the one." The exercise below can assist you.

Choose five qualities or features in descending order that you value most in a partner. For instance, neat, amusing, adventurous, considerate, emotionally open, athletic, attractive and stylish, protective, creative, chatty, clever, affectionate, monetarily successful, well-known, well-respected, popular charismatic, maternal/paternal, spiritual, nurturing, empowering Contemplate whether each attribute energizes, relaxes, or stirs you emotionally as you consider it. Is it a happy, bad, or neutral experience? A desire will be transitory or shallow, whereas a need will elicit a deeper emotional response. Repeat the activity to better grasp the distinctions between your desires and your felt needs in love. Is the person you think you're in love with the ability to meet these requirements?

IMPROVING FAMILY RELATIONSHIPS WITH EMOTIONAL INTELLIGENCE

In the family, emotional intelligence is important. There's nothing quite like being surrounded by family. Blood and marriage relatives are intended to be our closest allies, our most reliable providers of affection and support. On the other hand, our connections with family are frequently marred by misunderstanding and hate, as well as fighting and badgering. Those we should get to know and be known by the most become adversaries or strangers.

Our first and greatest emotional memories are formed in our families, and they continue to appear there. Emotional intelligence (EQ) succeeds where other family harmony efforts have failed. The ability to be attentive, accepting, and permanently attuned to ourselves and others—active awareness and empathy—tells us how to respond to one another's needs.

EQ is extremely useful in the family because it gives you control over your relationships with your parents and children, siblings, in-laws, and extended family. Other people's emotions can't manipulate you if you know how you feel, and you can't put family problems on everyone else if you know how you feel. Because close relationships are based on feelings, most approaches for enhancing family connections focus on communicating your sentiments to those you care about.

Family contact becomes a hardship without this emotional intimacy because no one wants to spend that much time with a stranger. You must start with your emotional honesty and openness if you want your family members to know and embrace each other lovingly. When you do, the tips below convert from common sense advice into incredibly effective ways to bring your family closer together.

METHODS FOR ENHANCING FAMILY INTERACTIONS WITH A HIGH EQ

1. **Look in the mirror first.**

A family is a system of interdependent individuals, but it doesn't mean you can blame your biological family for who you are now; you can blame your spouse and children for your pleasure. Your best chance of resolving any family issue is to focus on your emotional well-being. Your family will notice that your emotional independence helps not only you but also the entire family. They may rapidly follow your lead if you act on the notion that you have the right and obligation to assert your emotional demands.

2. **Keep in mind that regularity breeds trust.**

Lack of consistency, according to studies, weakens confidence. Those who love and rely on you, especially youngsters, will be puzzled and scared if you have sporadic emotional awareness. That is why it is critical to maintain your awareness with your family.

3. **Recognize that being close does not imply that you are identical twins.**

Family ties can sometimes obscure the distinctiveness of persons we care about. It's easy to forget that when you're proud of your family. You can't expect to have the same talents as your siblings, even though you look a lot similar; you can't expect to follow your parents' path, and you can't expect to spend all of your free time with your spouse simply because you're married.

4. **Remember that just because you've known someone your whole life doesn't imply you understand them.**

No matter how much I've always loved you, "I knew you when..." doesn't mean I know you today. We all change, yet we only appear to notice changes in ourselves. It's annoying to be introduced as someone's younger brother when you're fifty-five or to be treated like the nerd you were when you were fourteen, even though you're now the CEO of your firm. You can gently steer your family away from static patterns of interaction now that you've gained empathy by modeling the attention you'd like to receive. Don't fall back on the conversational safe haven of reminiscing about the past when you're with your family. By eliciting specifics and then listening with your body and thoughts, you can demonstrate that you are interested in what's new.

5. Keep an eye out for negative emotional recollections.

It's easy to feel weak and frustrated when you catch your thirty-year-old self responding to a parent in the voice of a five-year-old. You don't have to get snared by emotional recollections if you use EQ. Reflect on the memories that are imposing on your behavior today whenever you feel out of control with family—whether you're kicking yourself for acting like a child with your parents or agonizing over where the anger you're dumping on your innocent spouse and children is coming from.

6. Each family member should treasure each stage of life.

Even though we know it's impossible, we sincerely want Mom and Dad to stay the way they are and the kids to stay at home forever. Emotionally, the greatest way to accept that fact is to embrace change. Accept your parents' normal fear of aging, but utilize your emotional awareness and empathy to figure out ways to treasure this moment for its unique traits. What can you and your parents share today that you couldn't before? Can you keep having fun while ensuring that everyone in the family support system feels valuable and worthy, even if roles and duties must change?

7. Ask if you're unsure what will work.

Accepting your fear of change can make it easier to talk about topics that you might have avoided in the past. Perhaps your parents are just waiting for you to say anything. Examine them. Change is only one of the many ways you can enhance each other in a flexible, healthy family dynamic.

TO GET ALONG WITH OLDER RELATIVES, USE EMOTIONAL INTELLIGENCE.

Lack of time and many emotional memories jeopardize harmonious relationships with parents and adult siblings, in-laws, and adult children. The two add up to a concern that we'll be overwhelmed by each other's wants and sacrifice ourselves if we provide anything to these grown-up relatives. We do need to devote time to figuring out what our parents want most from us, maintaining tight friendships with brothers and sisters, and meeting together without succumbing to every awful joke about squabbling. These greedy families have ever been made.

However, because emotional intelligence provides us with so much energy and creativity, the expectations of these connections do not have to be high. When emotional memories are awakened, we can perceive change as it occurs in individuals. Maintain a high EQ, and your adult family interactions will no longer be dominated by cleaning up after mistakes and dealing with crises that have already turned into disasters.

IMPROVING YOUR ADULT CHILDREN'S CONNECTIONS

Many parents are disappointed to learn that they cannot simply sit back and enjoy the results of their labor after their children have reached adulthood. There is no such thing as a static relationship. Dealing with the change and growth that occurs before role reversal is crucial to maintaining a strong continuous connection with your grown children. You must maintain open lines of emotional connection with your children; at this moment in their lives, they may be preoccupied with their careers, loves, and friendships. Let them know how you're feeling and what you require.

Of course, if you've only recently boosted your EQ, you may need to adjust to your child-interaction style. Have you listened to your children's feelings regarding their decisions with empathy? Do they avoid you because you give them advice or make your own decisions? Do you bring into the relationship more disappointment and judgment than they can handle? Have you tried to figure out what their specific requirements are? Some adult children maintain their distance because previous interactions with you have hurt them; in this instance, the only way to mend the relationship is to follow these guidelines: listen to their pain and accept you were wrong.

Here are some ideas for bridging the gap:

You can still conduct this activity on your own if your child is unwilling to ask you are unwilling to ask. Fill out the list for yourself, then go to a different chair or position and complete the list as you would for your adult child. Now compare the two. Is your adult child's requirement different from what you're providing? Have you neglected to notice the changes in the child?

Taking back your adult siblings

In high-EQ households, brothers and sisters share responsibility for aging parents and look forward to opportunities to bring all generations together because they all understand their own limitations and strengths and how to communicate them. Unfortunately, because history often intervenes, this is not a true portrayal of many adult sibling relationships. Perhaps your parents didn't provide the same level of love and support for your brother as they did for you.

Perhaps childhood memories elicit excessive bitterness, jealousy, and rivalry. Maybe it was simply too much for you when your sister, who knew you so well, didn't see how much you'd changed over the years.

Whatever the issue, any of the suggestions in this article can help you renew your connection. If you have the time, reconnecting with your partner can also be accomplished by traveling somewhere together where you will both feel comfortable and undisturbed. Use your time together in an unstructured situation to convey many "I feel" messages. Make it clear that you're not wanting your sibling to change by expressing yourself. When your sibling responds, listen with your body rather than your head, and don't respond with retorts prepared beforehand.

Can you reconnect with your sibling by asking for aid in a way that honors their distinct talents if an outing isn't working? Consider how you may make your sibling feel especially needed.

IMPROVING YOUR EXTENDED FAMILY RELATIONSHIPS

What's the state of your extended family, whether you're related through marriage or by looser blood ties? You're exhausted because you're attempting to build family relationships without the necessary emotional history? Or are they smooth because they don't come with the emotional baggage that your extended family does? In any individual connection, either is conceivable. The difficulty of a relationship may be determined by how important it is to you and how long you've been together. Getting along with a new mother-in-law, and therefore mother, has left a bad taste in my mouth. On the other hand, being nice to the cousin you only see at holiday gatherings is surely a piece of cake.

What you want out of your extended family ties will determine how wonderful and deep they are. We feel bad if we resent our parents, but there's no law requiring us to love our in-laws, so many don't feel forced to go out of their way. Simply apply the same empathy to your extended family as you would to anybody else you meet, which involves recognizing the wide range of differences that will inevitably exist so you may find common ground.

You have a good chance of becoming everyone's favorite niece, cherished uncle, or model in-law if you're also willing to listen with empathy no matter who is speaking, confess fault, and watch your nonverbal signs. If you haven't yet reached that point, here are some suggestions for making extended-family interactions more fulfilling.

It's important to keep in mind that you don't have to like everyone equally.

Consider how much your own baggage prevents you from enjoying this individual. Even when you try your hardest to be open-hearted, you may develop a dislike for a family or in-law. Accept your emotions and simply interact with the person to the extent that you are comfortable. You might find that removing the tension of meeting them under duress widens the break in your heart.

Don't say anything if you can only ask loaded questions.

According to research, the emotional message accounts for 90% of what people take away from any conversation. This is why it's critical to be emotionally aware of your motivations and accept responsibility for what you communicate through gestures and expressions, and words. We are sometimes frightened to take responsibility for the feelings that motivate us, so we don't state what we mean. As a result, we manipulate people by offering offers that beg to be denied or by claiming that we don't mind when we do and then resenting the alleged offender. Go somewhere else if you can't be emotionally honest with your extended relatives.

HOW TO NURTURE EMOTIONAL INTELLIGENCE IN RELATIONSHIPS

Do you ever wonder how happy married couples manage to keep their happiness? Happy couples, it turns out, are very much the same as any other pair. They get into heated debates. They are under pressure at work. They are having difficulty raising their children. Difficult family problems arise, and couples frequently disagree. So, what distinguishes happily married couples? What keeps them somewhat content and happy?

Emotions are a powerful force that, for better or worse, sets the tone for a marriage. A better ability for emotional intelligence (EQ) in their relationship is one crucial feature that separates happily married couples from unhappily married couples.

In their regular interactions with one another, happy couples use emotional intelligence. They courteously conduct themselves when discussing topics. They pay attention. Their positive interactions outnumber their negative encounters by a significant margin. They frequently exhibit appreciation, comprehension, and respect for one another.

These attributes foster a favorable emotional climate that fosters feelings of connection, intimacy, and overall happiness and fulfillment.

Meta-emotions, or how you feel about your feelings, impact how you connect with your relationship. Suppose you were taught as a child that unpleasant feelings are bad and that expressing them is discouraged. In that case, you might find yourself minimizing or avoiding confrontation as much as possible or ignoring your feelings and working hard to please others. Uncomfortable negative emotions like anger, fear, or hurt are useful indicators that something is wrong and needs to be addressed. Avoiding these strong emotions simply serves to amplify their negative impact on you and your relationship, making it more difficult to deal with when they resurface.

Commit to recognizing, understanding, and communicating your feelings without resorting to blame, criticism or judgment.

Here are a few techniques to nurture your relationship's emotional intelligence:

Commit to recognizing, understanding, and communicating your feelings without resorting to blame, criticism or judgment. Negative emotions aren't the problem; it's how they're expressed that can be. When unpleasant feelings arise, take a break, calm yourself, and then return your attention to your spouse to talk about it. This will almost certainly result in increased connection and understanding between you and an increase in your relationship's degree of satisfaction and happiness.

EMOTIONAL INTELLIGENCE IN RELATIONSHIPS: HOW TO NURTURE IT

Emotional intelligence can be developed at any age. Any type of learning necessitates insight, so we must be aware of which component of emotional intelligence we should focus on.

It takes patience and time to develop emotional intelligence in relationships — EQ is a talent you must practice as you and your emotions change and mature. As clinical as it may sound, healthy relationships are ones in which partners actively work on themselves and have each other's backs.

I've compiled some advice on how to work with emotional intelligence and the simple but critical steps you can take to improve emotional intelligence in your relationships.

1. **Recognize all of your feelings for your companion.**

Yes, we know that The Beatles said that love is all you need, and it's true that love should be your primary emotion in your relationship. On the other hand, our feelings alter, evolve, and mutate as dynamic, deeply human beings.

Yes, you'll have unexpected mutant feelings toward your partner, such as contempt, resentment, wrath, and so on, and you'll be surprised and try to push them down.

"Now, we love each other, yet there are some aspects of each other that drive us insane." Jenny says, "I've been with my partner, Chris, for seven years." I find it disrespectful that he is never on time. He believes I'm way too worried about being on time. "There are times when I question whether love is enough to bring our lives together, and the truth is that it isn't. We needed to sit down and recognize that our feelings for each other aren't always great. And that's fine as long as love is at the center."

It's a depressing reality, but we don't always love the people. We have a lot of other sentiments for them, and it's important that we feel them all when it comes to building emotional intelligence in relationships.

2. Accept change as a part of your relationship.

I'm a wimp when it comes to change, and it takes me a long time to prepare and adjust. Change in a loving partnership, which is all about stability, can be scary when it's difficult to adapt to individual changes.

In a relationship, though, resisting change is both futile and harmful. Age, circumstance, geography, job changes, health concerns, and various other factors all affect relationships. For example, having a child can alter your marriage. Alternatively, your relationship could begin with a focus on passion and physical closeness. Other factors, such as companionship, friendship, and a sense of collaboration, may take precedence as you continue your journey together.

Allow things to flow rather than panicking at the first sign of change. The change will happen whether you like it or not, so the only thing you can do now is to decide how you'll deal with it. Working with emotional intelligence in relationships comes into play here.

Remember that multiple types of emotional intelligence exist, and which one you use will depend on where you are in your relationship. Emotional intelligence will differ from emotional intelligence in a fresh relationship in a marriage. Don't become a control freak; embrace change and be amazed at how much easier things become.

3. Share what you've learned.

A healthy, emotional relationship is built on sharing experiences and emotional understanding.

Any relationship, including high emotional intelligence, requires understanding that your spouse may have emotional intelligence components that you do not and vice versa. For example, you may be a better listener than they are, but they better manage their emotions.

"Even when we dispute, my partner is mindful about what he says and strives to avoid unpleasant language," Jason adds. "However, he isn't the most sympathetic guy and is unable to put himself in my shoes." I'm the polar opposite – I understand where he's coming from, but I'm also irritable, so I don't express things carefully."

Jason and his partner recognized that they had a lot to learn and aimed to absorb each other's strengths without becoming insecure. They also endeavor to guarantee that learning from one another does not degenerate into leeching one other's emotional energy in the spirit of high emotional intelligence.

Action is needed to emphasize the value of emotional intelligence in relationships, and actively learning from each other is one of the most important things you can do.

4. **If you're terrified, acknowledge it; if you're unsure, ask.**

Another crucial aspect of emotional intelligence is honesty. When you're afraid of something, admit it, and be honest when you're unsure. There will never be a love affair without dread or uncertainty, and you must be able to express both of these emotions healthily.

Remember that it's always a good idea to inquire if you're unsure when it comes to consent. Consent is required in all situations, not just in the bedroom. If you think looking through a partner's desk intrudes on their privacy, ask first, or ask yourself if you need to.

Also, express what you're terrified of. For example, if you have abandonment fears due to childhood trauma or toxic parents, talk to your partner about it. Talk to your partner if you think you might require treatment to deal with these anxieties. Whether it's emotional intelligence in a 15-year marriage or a brand-new relationship, honesty rarely fails when delivered honestly and softly."

WHAT ACTIONS AND BEHAVIORS WILL MAKE OUR RELATIONSHIP HEALTHIER?

Teaching and developing social and emotional intelligence has been increasingly popular. Social and emotional learning (SEL) programs are already commonplace in many schools.

These programs are designed to help children improve their health and well-being while supporting academic performance and reducing bullying. In everyday life, emotional intelligence can be applied in various ways.

- **Before you react, think first.**

Emotionally savvy people understand that emotions can be powerful but fleeting. When a highly charged emotional event occurs, such as being enraged at a coworker, the emotionally wise answer is to wait. This allows everyone to settle down and think more clearly about all issues.

- **Self-awareness is a good thing.**

Emotionally intelligent people are skilled at imagining how others could feel, but they are also skilled at comprehending their own emotions. People with self-awareness can consider all of the things that influence their feelings. Emotionally intelligent people are acutely aware of their emotions, even negative ones like frustration or sadness. They can recognize and comprehend their feelings, and name an emotion aids in its management. As a result, the emotionally intelligent have high self-esteem and are realistic in their assessments.

- **Other-centered empathy**

Being able to consider and sympathize with how other people are experiencing is an important aspect of emotional intelligence. This frequently entails thinking about how you would react in a similar situation.

People with strong emotional intelligence may consider other people's perspectives, experiences, and feelings and use that information to justify their actions.

Emotional awareness is critical, but what can you do to improve your social and emotional skills?

Tips to get you started

Listen

Paying attention is the first step in understanding what other people are going through. Take the time to pay attention to what others are attempting to say to you, both orally and nonverbally. The meaning of one's body language is quite important. Consider the various things that could be contributing to someone's mood when you sense that they are feeling a specific way.

Empathize

Empathize with others as much as possible. It's critical to read people's emotions, but you must also be able to put yourself in their position to comprehend what they're going through genuinely. Such activities can help you acquire a deeper emotional knowledge of a situation over time and stronger emotional skills. The empathic are often supportive of the people in their lives, and they can readily change their feelings to match another person's mood.

A person with a high EQ can hear and understand the viewpoints of others clearly. This person can recognize and understand other people's emotions, which is a skill related to empathy.

Reflect

Emotional intelligence is defined by the ability to reason with emotions. Consider how your feelings affect your choices and actions. Consider the role that emotions play in how other people respond.

RISKS TO AVOID

Low emotional intelligence can lead to many problems in life, including work and relationships. People with fewer emotional skills are more likely to get into fights, have poorer relationships, and have trouble coping with their emotions.

Learn to notice and understand your emotions to begin. If you can name the emotion you're feeling, you'll have a greater chance of understanding what you're going through. Stopping and thinking before behaving or judging might also help you improve your emotional regulation. These skills will help you cultivate an inner martial resolve and maintain your concentration on the vital things in life.

When logic and emotions are considered simultaneously, we make the best decisions. When our emotions take precedence over our logic, we may take actions not in our best interests.

MAINTAINING AN HEALTHY RELATIONSHIP

Unlike vacation love stories and romantic comedies, maintaining successful relationships takes some effort when everything is resolved after one or two disagreements. It does not, however, have to be tough.

It's exhausting to keep up with all of life's responsibilities—work, kids, family, friends, neighbors, and your home—and many of us are simply exhausted. It's reasonable that dealing with partner issues goes to the bottom of your priority list, given the daily grind of duties and frayed nerves. It's easy to postpone tackling your stalled relationship or eroded intimacy concerns, especially during trying times.

Be a good listener, carve out time together, enjoy a decent sex life, and divide up those bothersome chores, to name a few tried-and-true strategies for improving relationships. While relationship experts have found them successful, you can also try these seven novel techniques to bond and strengthen your relationship.

Take some time apart

Take a vacation from your mate, which may seem contradictory as a strategy to enhance your relationship. Outside of a partnership, everyone requires their own space and quality time. Counselors in dating and marriage remind us that you are entitled to some breathing room.

When intimacy collapses into fusion, it is not a lack of connection that stifles desire but rather too much closeness. Our need for unity coexists with our desire for separation. As a result, separation is a requirement for connection: this is the central paradox of intimacy and sex.

Individuals require alone time for personal development and independence when in a relationship. Individuals flourish, and the relationship as a whole benefits. It's crucial to a happy marriage.

Do something alone, whether reading or going for a walk in the park. Perhaps you'd like to go for a workout with a friend.

As a result, your partner's annoying tendencies will irritate you less. You'll notice that you're feeling more energized and patient. Your particular companion misses you as well.

Other advantages: you'll contribute more to the relationship as a whole. Regularly taking a break keeps your time together from becoming stale. Instead, it promotes curiosity, more intriguing conversations, and personal development. Taking time apart will, in effect, revitalize the partnership dynamic.

Go to Bed and Get Up at the Same Time

You may have heard that most adults in the United States do not get the seven to eight hours of healthful sleep they require each night. Did you realize, though, that going to bed at separate times hurts you and your partner?

Head to bed at the same time for a healthier connection. Some work in bed while the other watches Netflix in another room, and there are others who work in bed while the other watch Netflix in another room. Regardless of the circumstance, keep your bedtimes in sync.

Seventy-five percent of couples don't go to bed together, according to Chris Brantner, a certified sleep science coach, which has detrimental consequences. Those who have different sleep schedules have more conflict, less talk, and less sex than those who go to bed together.

This does not permit you to hide beneath the covers and surf through social media when both of you are in bed.

Screen Time Has an Effect on Couples. According to a Pew Research poll, respondents are upset by their partners' use of mobile devices:

Make Yourself Vulnerable

To be vulnerable, you sometimes have to dig deep. "It may surprise couples, but if each of them becomes curious about their blind spots, discovers them, and then is brave enough to express that vulnerability, it can help establish deeper intimacy," said Meredith Resnick, LCSW, creator of Shamerecovery.com.

"A blind spot isn't always a flaw or a weakness," Resnick continued, "but rather a deeply held idea about oneself, how a relationship is supposed to work, or how love is presented." The notion is so ingrained in us that we aren't even aware of it, hence the "blind spot."

What is an example of a relationship's blind spots? "For instance, one partner might realize that their inclination to micromanage people is tied to their fear of abandonment—controlling a loved one's schedule as a way never to be alone," explains Resnick.

"Sharing this with a partner is a good way to change this pattern." "This should be a compassionate, trust-building process, not a shame-inducing one," adds Resnick.

Make Unique Experiences

Boredom can sneak in, even though eating your favorite pizza every Saturday night and incorporating traditions into your life enriches relationships. As a result, you should mix things up by adding unpredictable date evenings and enjoyable moments to your routine.

According to relationship specialist, lecturer, and author Terri Orbuch, Ph.D., it is critical to maintain spontaneity in a marriage even after many years.

Can you buy a trampoline or do something surprising instead of going on an adventure like rock climbing or learning a new language? Perhaps you can find additional methods to revitalize your connection.

Focus on novelty, variation, and surprise, according to psychologists. According to research, participants rekindled their love and felt closer following weeks of intriguing dates.

Little Things Can Surprise You

Couples that are happy with one other are kind to each other. Small gestures maintain the flame and remind your lover that you are thinking of them. It's a plus if you can help out by donating or volunteering. In reality, random acts of kindness can have a big impact, boosting general happiness.

Respect your partner's preferred method of communication. They hug you, for example, because they value physical contact. Because you appreciate acts of service and quality time together, you'd be even pleased if they tidied up the living room or spent more time away from their workstation. Learn how to express your love so that your partner values your relationship.

Suggestions for Surprising Your Partner in a Fight

While no one wants to dispute with someone they care about, arguments can benefit. It's how you fight, and it matters if you fight fairly and constructively.

Rolling your eyes or expressing scorn are the worst things you can do. So, what is it that works?

Soften the Launch

Your tone and intent are the most important factors to consider. Softly and gently speak. Politeness goes a long way in our world. The important thing is to talk without blaming others. Avoid making a defensive or critical reply that could intensify a quarrel."

HOW CAN WE PREVENT CRITICISM, MANIPULATION, AND BLAME GAMES IN RELATIONSHIPS?

The majority of individuals react in ways that increase abuse or play into the abuser's hands, making them feel tiny and bad, but they retreat and allow inappropriate behavior to continue. Many of us aren't even aware that we're being duped. We may have an uneasy gut feeling that contradicts the manipulator's remarks, or we may feel compelled to comply with a request. Because you've had a manipulative parent, it may be more difficult to spot in a spouse.

The ancient notion of "knowing your enemy" is crucial when dealing with a manipulator. You can respond strategically to covert manipulation if you recognize these concealed arrows. Knowing what they're up to gives you power.

Aggressive behavior occurs when someone attacks you overtly or secretly. What appears to be passive or defensive behavior when people act passive-aggressively is actually covert aggressiveness. It's debatable if their actions are deliberate or unintentional. It makes no difference to the victim. The result is identical. Being excessively sympathetic puts you at risk of being abused repeatedly.

Psychologist George Simon claims that these covert manipulators say and do things on purpose to gain power and influence. He claims that the techniques of typically unstable people, such as sociopaths and narcissists, and some persons with borderline personality disorder, aren't unconscious in the manner that defense mechanisms generally operate. On the other hand, their behavior has been so ingrained that it has become reflexive over time. They don't even realize it, but they are aware of it.

MANIPULATOR'S OBJECTIVES

All manipulation seeks to obtain influence to meet our wants, but persistent manipulators seek power and control by employing deceitful and abusive tactics. Manipulators retain dominance by using emotional manipulation, abuse, and coercion regularly. They're frequently passive-aggressive. To deflect any criticism and continue to behave inappropriately, they may lie or act caring, upset, or horrified by your criticisms. Manipulators seek to maintain control so that they can do whatever they want:

You may eventually become a victim and lose faith in yourself, your feelings, and your senses. Gaslighting is a deceptive and debilitating form of deception.

Tactical Manipulation in the Dark

Overt aggressiveness, such as criticism, narcissistic abuse, and subtle types of emotional abuse, are all examples of manipulation. Guilt, complaining, comparing, lying, denying, feigning ignorance or innocence (e.g., "Who me!?"), blame, bribery, undermining, mind games, assumptions, "foot-in-the-door," reversals, emotional blackmail, evasiveness, forgetting, inattention, fake concern, sympathy, apologies, flattery, and gifts and favors are among manipulators' favorite covert weapons. "How to Recognize Manipulation" is a good place to start. The following are some examples of typical tactics:

Lying

Those who are habitual liars may lie when it is not necessary. They're lying not out of fear or remorse but to perplex you and get you to do what they want. Some use accusations and other manipulative tactics to put you on the defensive simultaneously. Lying can also take the form of vagueness and omission of material information, even if the rest of what is said is truthful. A cheater, for example, can claim that they were working late or at the gym but not admit to having had an adulterous encounter.

Denial

This isn't unconscious denial, such as failing to recognize that you've been abused, have an addiction, or avoid painful truths. This is deliberate denial to deny knowledge of pledges, agreements, and actions. Minimization, rationalization, and justifications are all forms of denial. To make you doubt yourself or win compassion, the manipulator acts as if you're making a big issue out of nothing or rationalizes and explains their behavior.

Avoidance

Manipulators will go to any length to avoid being faced and taking responsibility. They may refuse to explain their behavior to avoid having to talk about it. This could be used with an assault, such as "You're always bothering me," to put you on the defensive by blaming, guilting, or shaming you.

When a manipulator alters the subject, avoidance might be subtle and unnoticed. It could be hidden by boasting, flattery, or statements you want to hear, such as "You know how much I care about you." You may forget why you're irritated in the first place.

Evasiveness is another avoidance tactic that clouds the truth, confuses you, and sows doubt. I once dated a man who claimed we couldn't get along because I was too meticulous, and he was a "gloss-over" type of person. Precisely! When I asked him questions or pointed out discrepancies in his half-truths, he became irritated. It became clear that he was a devious, talented liar. If you have any doubts, believe them! When you're hopeful about a relationship, it's easy to give someone the benefit of the doubt and fall into denial yourself.

Blame, Shame, and Guilt

Projection is a defense in which the manipulator accuses others of their behavior. "The best defense is a good offense," say manipulators. The offended party is now on the defensive due to the blame shift. The manipulator stays free to continue, while their victims are now filled with guilt and shame.

Abusers frequently point the finger at their victims or anyone else. Be skeptical of an apology that is nothing more than a ruse. Addicts frequently blame others for their addiction, such as their demanding boss or "bitchy" spouse. When a criminal defendant has no defense, they will criticize the police and their techniques of gathering evidence. Rapists used to be able to harm their victims' reputations.

In a domestic violence situation, I counseled a couple in which the violent husband blamed his wife for his aggression. "I'm amazed your wife has that much control over you," I told him. He was taken aback, for his entire plan had been to gain influence over her.

Guilt-tripping and humiliating shift the spotlight to you, weakening you while empowering the abuser. When Martyrs say or imply, "After all, I've done for you...", it's often accompanied by criticism that you're selfish or ungrateful.

Shaming makes you feel inept by going beyond guilt. It degrades you as a person, your characteristics, or function, rather than just your conduct. "If the children had a father who knew how to parent (or made a reasonable living), they would behave." Comparing is a subtle yet effective type of humiliation. When parents compare siblings to each other or playmates, it is damaging. Some spouses compare their partners to their ex-partners to get an advantage by making their partners feel inferior.

"Blaming the victim" is one kind of guilt and humiliation. For example, you discover proof of flirting on your partner's phone. Your partner is furious that you used the phone. They have now shifted the spotlight to you. Your partner has avoided a confrontation over flirting by blaming you and may even lie about it, diminish it, or avoid it entirely by blaming you. You, the true victim, will feel terrible for spying, which will subdue any legitimate rage and allow the flirting to continue unabated.

Intimidation

Threats aren't always used to intimidate people; they can also be subtle. Intimidation can be performed by using a certain attitude or tone, as well as words such as "I always get my way;" "No one is indestructible." "The grass doesn't seem to be getting any greener;" "I have high-ranking friends and methods;" "You're not so young anymore," or "Have you thought about the consequences of your decision?" Another method is to give a fear-inducing scenario: "She left her husband and lost her children, their home, and everything." "I'm in it to win it." "Once upon a time, I was on the verge of killing a man."

Acting as a Victim

This is not the same as blaming the victim. Rather than blaming you, this "poor me" strategy instills guilt and pity in you, causing you to do their bidding. "If you don't help me, I'm not sure what I'll do." If you leave, more unstable personalities frequently threaten suicide. It can also mean, "You don't care about me;" or "You don't care about me;" or "You don't care about me;" or "You don't "Why do you treat me this way?" or "No one is willing to aid me." Your cooperation fosters animosity, undermines the connection, and invites manipulation to persist. Irrational guilt is guilt about someone else's behavior or predicament.

These strategies are harmful. Don't get the two mixed up. Forgiveness is not the same as forgetting. Manipulation is almost certain to continue. This is traumatic over time and can seriously harm your self-esteem. The first step is to become aware of the problem. You may require assistance to see things. Make a list of all the discussions you have and figure out who is abusing you and what strategies are being utilized. Even more difficult to not take the manipulator's statements personally and learn how to respond. Learn how to deal with a narcissist and difficult people and how to assert yourself and set boundaries.

Childhood trauma is frequently what causes you to reject and become vulnerable to abuse in the first place. If your self-worth has been harmed, you may need to Conquer Shame.

HOW TO DEVELOP AND EXPR EMPATHY FOR YOUR PARTNER.

Empathy is a strong force that promotes social harmony and collaboration. It's the system that allows people to comprehend and relate to one another. Empathy is a prerequisite for closeness, trust, and a sense of belonging. It's also the feeling that makes it tough to ignore other people's pain.

Empathic persons get a variety of happiness benefits. Empathy has been shown to increase cooperation and forgiveness, strengthen relationships, decrease aggression and judgment, and even improve mental and physical health. Empathy-based kindness has been shown to increase cooperation and forgiveness, strengthen relationships, decrease aggression and judgment, and even improve mental and physical health.

Interestingly, despite rating themselves as more empathic, happier people are less conscious of unpleasant emotions in others, according to studies. However, regardless of our mood, it is critical to developing empathy to increase our own and others' happiness.

The fundamental elements of empathy can help you better understand and communicate with people in your life if you practice them.

Make it a priority to listen.

You must first recognize what someone else is feeling before connecting with them. Listening is important, but it isn't always easy.

When a close friend calls to whine about how hectic work has been or how difficult things have been since their recent breakup, the intensity in their voice generally catches your attention right away. It's even more difficult when conversations take place amid distractions and have less visible emotional weight.

Setting the intention to listen for emotion is the first step toward empathy. Attempt to identify people's signals that might indicate how they're feeling.

When it comes to noticing what others are feeling, your own emotions might be a huge obstacle. When you're having a discussion and thinking about your sentiments and how to express them, you might not be paying attention to what's going on on the other end. Making an effort to listen actively might help you better grasp emotions and empathy.

Their Emotions Are Shared

Empathy puts you in another person's shoes after you recognize their emotion. Empathy isn't about feeling how you would like in that circumstance; it's about putting yourself in their shoes for a few moments and adopting their feelings.

According to some research, mirror neurons, or brain connections that fire whether we're experiencing the stimulus or seeing someone else experience it, may help us excel at this job.

Mirror neurons get your heart pounding when you see athletes dashing through a stadium at your favorite sporting event or make you cringe in agony when you see unfortunate gaffes in a funny viral video.

When people become involved in another person's grief, sadness, or frustration, empathy allows them to stand with them and console them with deeper understanding, but it also conveys a message that they are prepared to take on an unpleasant emotion so that others can do not have to.

Create a Vulnerable Situation for Yourself

Empathic ties are reciprocal. Allowing yourself to absorb another person's emotion fully can strengthen your bonds, and allowing yourself to be vulnerable to others can increase such bonds.

When you disclose your own difficult emotions, such as guilt, fear, and shame, you allow others to sympathize with you.

In two ways, being vulnerable enhances your empathy. First, seeing the importance of empathy when returned to you helps strengthen your commitment to empathize with others. You'll also feel more at ease handling difficult emotions in social situations.

It's not easy to keep a conversation about painful feelings going. Still, if you intentionally train yourself to seize opportunities when you have an emotion to share, you'll be more prepared for the receiving end.

Take Action and Offer Assistance

If empathy is based on sharing bad emotions, happiness may decrease. People grow closer to placing themselves in other people's shoes when they experience genuine compassion for victims of natural disasters.

However, simply feeling another's grief, while it may increase a sense of belonging and understanding if shared, does not maximize the possibility to improve one's well-being. Knowing what another person is going through gives you an advantage in determining what they require.

Because empathy entails adopting the emotion but not the difficult situation that caused it, you are usually better positioned to assist.

It is necessary to feel both the anguish of another and the knowledge that you are in a position to help them for empathy to be most effective and optimize well-being.

Participants with effective empathy felt enough of the shock's anguish to desire to help, but not so much that they were hesitant to take it on themselves.

Empathy-Inducing Techniques

Practice the following regularly to improve your empathy. You'll notice that your ability to comprehend and relate to other people's emotions improves.

Empathy allows you to not only understand others but can also provide you with the motivation to make a difference. Empathy becomes successful when you utilize it to motivate you to do something about the problem, whether it's consoling a buddy, buying a small present for someone who needs it, or donating to causes that support natural disaster victims.

When you observe someone else going through a difficult moment, listen and offer your thoughts and figure out what you can do to help. The empathy that is followed through entails promoting good change for others. The wonderful thing about empathy is that it improves your own life and the lives of others.

CONCLUSION

In a word, emotional intelligence is the ability to detect and control our own emotions, to understand and feel empathy for the feelings of others, and to use these abilities to communicate effectively and form healthy, productive relationships with others. Healthy, productive relationships are important not only for our mental health but also for our physical well-being.

While some academics believe emotional intelligence can be taught and improved, others believe it is a natural trait. Thankfully, emotional intelligence isn't a one-size-fits-all trait. You may develop your emotional intelligence by applying your head and heart to the work.

Psychologists refer to this capacity as emotional intelligence. It's critical to be able to express and control one's emotions, but it's equally critical to identify, analyze, and respond to the emotions of others. Imagine being unable to discern whether a buddy or a coworker was dissatisfied.

In numerous scientific research, numerous scientific research, positive emotions have been linked to better health, a longer lifespan, and a greater sense of well-being. Chronic anger, worry, and hate, on the other hand, raise people's blood pressure and tighten their blood vessels, increasing their risk of heart disease. On the other hand, maintaining a healthy, happy emotional state is tough.

The emotionally intelligent can change gears and lighten the mood internally and externally. A person with a high EQ isn't rash or hasty in their decisions. They pause to consider their options before acting. This translates to consistent emotion regulation, or the ability to lower the intensity of emotion. Down-regulation is the process of reducing one's anger or anxiety. These people are particularly sensitive to the feelings of others. Understandably, being sensitive to emotional signals from within one's own body and social environment could help one be a better friend, parent, leader, or romantic partner. Others will have less work if you are in tune with them.

A person with a high EQ attracts us naturally. With their easy rapport, we feel relaxed and at ease. They appear to have a superhuman ability in reading social cues. They might even be able to read other people's minds. This effortlessness is appreciated at home, in social situations, and at work. Who wouldn't want a boss who understands your feelings and what you're trying to achieve?

Couples with flourishing, solid relationships are more likely to have developed emotional intelligence. The ability to be aware of, control, and express emotions healthy are referred to as emotional intelligence. In other words, it is the ability to manage relationships effectively and compassionately. Emotional intelligence in a relationship refers to being aware of both your own and your partner's emotions.

It's critical to grow our emotional intelligence as partners because emotionally intelligent couples can comprehend their connection; they grasp their responsibilities and identities as a pair and what generates negativity in the relationship." It makes us aware of the changes we or others are undergoing. Through emotional intelligence in relationships, people may develop stability and harmony.

In a relationship, those who lack emotional intelligence will rarely know what to say or what not to say." They can unintentionally say something insensitive that hurts the other partner. Furthermore, when a couple lacks emotional intelligence, they will continue to blame themselves if something goes wrong.

Also, if one spouse lacks emotional intelligence, recognizing how the other feels, expressing or honoring the emotional needs of the other partner may be difficult." And this could cause issues in the relationship. Perhaps one of the partners has a hard time accepting criticism. The partner may have difficulty resolving conflicts and interacting with loved ones.

Do Not Go Yet; One Last Thing To Do

If you enjoyed this book or found it useful, I'd be very grateful if you'd post a short review on Amazon. Your support does make a difference, and I read all the reviews personally so I can get your feedback and make this book even better.

Thanks again for your support!

Printed in Great Britain
by Amazon